God is a Feast

God is a Feast

A new look at

Saint John of the Cross

Father Pius Sammut
Discalced Carmelite

God is a Feast
Fr. Pius Sammut, O.C.D.
First published in Malta in 1992.

Translation © Mark Agius M.D., Luton, Beds
First published in Great Britain in 1996 by New Life
Publishing

ISBN   0-9529 159-0-1

Typeset in Times 12 pt - Gerald Vann, Tadworth
Cover design - Naomi Shannon, Oxted
Artwork - Andrew Lodge
Printed and bound - Staples, Rochester, Kent

Passages used and drawing of Christ
Crucified taken by permission of the
Institute of Carmelite Studies,
Washington D.C., U.S.A.

Sketch of St. John of the Cross facing
pages 9 and 232 by kind permission of
Andrew Lodge. London 1996

Translator's Preface

One usually translates something which one has found useful oneself - having found it useful, one feels that the same information might be useful to others.

I first came across St. John of the Cross when I was a General Practice Trainee at the Luton and Dunstable Hospital in 1978, doing work in psychiatry. I found mention of 'ecstasy' as a differential diagnosis of unusual mental states in a textbook of psychiatry and there St. Teresa of Avila and St. John of the Cross were mentioned as examples. I felt challenged to read their original writings in order to find out something about their state of mind. Soon, I had acquired and read all of their works. I was impressed enough by what I read to decide to join the Carmelite Third Order and to take as my 'name in religion', 'John of the Cross'.

However, I cannot say that I had 'interiorised' John's teaching until, in the summer of 1992, I met by chance Fr. Pius Sammut, O.C.D. He was, for me, a man in John's image - for indeed, John was his spiritual father. He was, and had been for several years, provincial of the Discalsed Carmelites in Malta. He later left this post to take up his present post as an evangelist in the United States and the Philippines, but throughout I have kept him as my spiritual director.

A short time later tragedy struck our parish when a young girl died of anorexia. I was not this family's G.P. but I felt moved to do what I could to bring comfort to the family. To find strength for myself and them and to find a meaning and a way forward in the faith in the midst of the stresses of life, I turned to Fr. Pius' book on John of the Cross, which had been a best seller in Maltese. Such concepts as the idea that "for the Christian, all things work together for good" seemed to give hope in the bleakest situations. The idea that God is totally in love with each one of us - to the extent of wishing to live within us, or to "espouse" us, offered a possibility of an empowerment of each one of us which must overcome all the obstacles of our life's path.

I found it difficult to express these concepts verbally to my friends and hence the idea emerged of translating the whole book into English.

Meanwhile, I have shared Pius' and St. John's ideas with many people. It has been hard work preparing the publishing of the book. My thanks must go to my wife, Anne, who has had great patience with the preparation of the manuscript, and also to Gerard and Toni Pomfret of New Life Publishing who have been immensely helpful. Many friends have encouraged me, and sharing with them has helped me in my own spiritual journey. By a strange twist in God's plan for me, I again find myself working in the psychiatric wing of the Luton and Dunstable Hospital.

To all those mentioned above and especially (they will know why) to my friends Teresa, Felicity, Helena, Marianne, Jeannie and Catherine, I dedicate this translation in the hope that it will say something to them as it has to me.

Mark Agius

15.8.96   Feast of the Assumption

INDEX

INDEX

□

Foreword

Have you ever been in love? asked the venerable old Abba of the latest young recruit to the community. When the young man simply answered *No,* the Abba dryly answered *Then, what did you come here for?*

This story illustrates the only problem with this book. If you have never experienced love in your life, if your heart has never been aflame with passion for someone .... then maybe it is better that you simply do not read this book because you may be scandalized! On the other hand, if at some stage in your life, love has set fire to your heart and inspired your mind ... this book will open new horizons for you.

This book is about a saint. His name is Fray Juan de la Cruz. Many Christians have never heard of him and of the few who have, many have been highly misinformed. He is not a living force in the imagination of the normal Christian. While Saint Augustine reminds us of the radical demands of the Gospel, Saint Francis typifies happiness in poverty, Saint Dominic demonstrates the power of preaching the Word of God, Saint Ignatius shows us the beauty of a life devoted to following God's will and the life of Saint Teresa of Avila (referred to in this book from now on as 'Our Holy Mother' as she is known in the Discalced Carmelite Order) is an illustration of the intimate depths of the life of prayer, Saint John of the Cross reminds us of nothing. Even worse, his name immediately brings to our mind thoughts of self-denial, penance and austerity of life. His *nada* - nothing - has certainly remained famous!

Why? Perhaps because of one small incident in his life which caught the imagination of those authors who wrote about him and those artists who painted him. The story is simple. Six months before he died, while he was in Segovia as prior of the monastery, he went out for a walk in the garden with his brother Francis. During the walk, he recounted an earlier episode. He said that a few months before, he had noticed a painting of Christ carrying the cross which was hanging in the corridor of the monastery.

It was a beautiful painting so he thought that it would be better to place it in the Church for the devotion of the people than to keep it hidden within the cloistered walls of the monastery. When he did this, he heard a voice asking him: *John, what do you wish me to do for you? And I answered him suffer and be humiliated for your sake. But apparently He has not taken much notice of what I said because I am being respected far too much over here....* John of the Cross concluded, smiling.

This expression *to suffer and be humiliated for you*, has been extended out of proportion as if it included the whole substance of the teaching of the saint. But, as anyone who is familiar with his life and his writings can easily deduct, this is a very partial and in a certain sense mistaken view.

We have no reason to be unduly surprised that many have misinterpreted him. Few understood him even when he was alive. *I cannot understand why no one remembers this saint* Mother Teresa of Jesus wrote angrily to Father Gracian! Many failed to assess his caliber correctly even after his death. For centuries this saint remained buried under the dust of indifference.

He began to be rehabilitated only at the beginning of this century when on the 24 August 1926 Pope Pius XI declared him a Doctor of the Church. Thus, at last, serious studies began to be made on his life and message.

It is enough to mention the Spanish Father Crisogono and the French Father Bruno, two Discalced Carmelite friars who have given us a new, more dynamic vision of the saint: no longer the awkward, timid friar enclosed in his monastic room, but a highly energetic person who was able to live the contemplative ideal amid the hurly-burly of life. Philosophers began to show an interest in him; the agnostic Jean Baruzzi and later the French Jacques Maritain launched him into the world of culture. Spanish, indeed world, literature suddenly realized that it had a poetic genius in its midst which had never been recognized.

Psychologists began studying the systematic way in which John of the Cross diagnoses the factors which condition and subdue man and the effective therapy which he offers so that man can live a life of freedom. Theologians stopped considering him as a mystic spiritual writer of no value and began to understand the deep intuitions of this man, especially all his theological reflections on faith, hope and love. Christianity is not an human struggle but a free gift.

During the Second Vatican Council, many prophesied that this saint would be eclipsed because of the Church's new emphasis on terrestrial values and social commitment. Today, the Christian is taught to involve himself in the social problems which agonize the world. But the opposite happened. Once more God bewildered the sociologist! Indeed, perhaps never more than today, has there been such an interest in this Saint.

In the religious circles we can take Pope John Paul II as a typical example of this new interest. As a young priest, in 1948, Carol Woytila wrote his doctoral thesis on Faith in Saint John of the Cross, and when later in 1982, as Pope, he visited the Saint's grave in Segovia he called this saint *a theologian, poet, artist, man of heaven, teacher of the faith, mystic doctor.*   In the literary sphere, the Mexican Ottavio Pas, Nobel Laureate of literature in 1990, stated that it was Saint John of the Cross who inspired him to write his best prose and poetry.

The discovery of Saint John of the Cross in modern times is naturally related to his intrinsic value as a poet and a mystic. But his message responds also to the deep needs of modern man. Man today finds himself very much in tune with this saint. John's concept of the *dark night,* the radical nature of his life and message, his realistic

4

attitude towards creation and the vision this man-of-God has of life, create a close affinity with the modern man who tries so hard to make sense of the ambiguity of his life. In Saint John of the Cross, man finds someone who understands him and, best of all, offers a way out of all this stress and anxiety.[1]

This Carmelite Saint has an important message for the culture of today because he offers a tenable answer to the questionings of contemporary man. His *stimulating and profound word,* helps us handle things without being manipulated, relate to people without exploiting them, enjoy everything without neglecting Him. As one of the early Fathers of the Church said: *God wants to mold us into sovereigns of the universe, brothers and sisters to all people, citizens of heaven, meek and humble servants.* Quite an ambitious venture! Nothing less can satisfy us! This is the main reason why I have written this book.

I have written it with much love and violence!

Love towards this friar who we, Discalced Carmelites, consider *teacher, father and guide.* We call him affectionately our *Holy Father.*

Violence because I feel that far too many people have a wrong understanding of God! Hence the name of the book **"God is a Feast"**. John of the Cross has taught me in the tranquility of my monastery room and in the intimacy of our chapel that God is neither a policeman nor a judge. He does not enjoy frightening people! He is Lover who is kind and caring, always dreaming of passion and tenderness.

He is not interested in laws and precepts. My God is pleased when we love him, not when we obey him. We are not androids. We are not slaves. We are persons who have a heart beating! Our God believes in love and not in the observance of commandments! *If a soul seeks God, even more so does the Bridegroom seek her; if she sends him her wishes of love, He sends her his inspirations and his divine touches. God's wish is to predispose her for more, even higher and delicate graces, which bring her closer to the divine nature, until she comes to take such a pure attitude that she will deserve union with God and complete change into him* ... Whoever builds a relationship with God finds his life moving gradually into a feast full of music.

The book is divided into four parts: **Life, Message, Writing, Celebration.** In writing his *Life,* I have tried to show the man who is Saint John of the Cross. The *Message* shows the profound affinity there is between our life with all its contradictions and the vision and message which this enamored mystic offers. His *Writings* introduce us to several short sentences which he himself wrote and handed to people who frequented him for spiritual direction - they are like sharp arrows which penetrate the marrow of our heart. The last section, *Celebration,* offers a few liturgical suggestions for those who wish to enjoy in an atmosphere of prayer, this God who Saint John of the Cross loved so much.

My hope and desire is that whoever reads this book will live the same adventure of love which this Saint enjoyed! You will discover that the **only** one who can make your heart overflow with joy, tenderness and zeal is this

God revealed to us in Jesus Christ! *Oh what the soul feels here, surrounded by such great favours! How she melts with love! What thanksgiving she gives when she sees God's heart open to her with such great and deep love! When she feels surrounded with all these divine pleasures, she gives herself completely to Him, and she too gives Him the breast of her will and her love.*

Please pray for me.[2]

Father Pius Sammut,

(Discalced Carmelite)

Tas-Silg Retreat House, Malta
Easter Sunday
19 April 1992

□

Introduction

Poet, Lover, Mystic [3]

It was the night between Friday and Saturday 14th of December 1591. Midnight has just struck when, in the monastery of Saint Miguel in Ubeda, Father Juan de la Cruz passed over to real life. Someone once remarked that death, perhaps, is the only moment in life when man is genuinely free because for the first time he is released from all social constraints and hence his true self, his real individuality can come out.

Hence this small incident, recounted to us by the leading biographer of the saint, Father Crisogono, acquires a lot of significance. When Father John was dying, a *conjunto* of musicians approached the window of his room and started singing and playing some popular melodies to relieve his mind of the pain. The intention of the musicians was laudable. But the sick Fray Juan confided with his friends that he could hardly hear them because he was listening to other melodies - melodies from heaven.

Later, just a few minutes before he died, following the normal ritual, the Prior began the litany of the Saints.

However Father John stopped him and told him: *Father, these are not necessary any more now. Please read for me some verses from the Song of Songs.* And, while listening to those passionate words of love between the bride and the bridegroom, he murmured *What precious pearls!!* His last words as soon as he heard the strokes of the bells announcing that it was time to chant Matins, were words of joy *I am going now to sing in Heaven! Me voy a cantar al cielo!*

This is Saint John of the Cross: music, passion, song. Here is a man who has a heart of a gracious artist. Sensitive, affectionate, tender. *He was always singing* avows the friar who accompanied him on his journeys between El Calvario and Beas. During the beatification process, another friar remembered: *When out walking, he would be so cheerful, especially when he found himself in the open country, that he would not feel the weariness of the journey and he used to show this joy by singing very devotional songs to Our Lady or to the Child Jesus or psalms of David or verses taken from the Song of Songs.*

For John of the Cross art is not a gratifying distraction, a treat for those who want to escape from the harsh realities of life and wander in a personal nirvana created by their imagination, but on the contrary, art is the way - perhaps the only way - by which man can unfold the intricacy of life in its true dimension, the divine dimension:

> *By the pleasant lyres*
> *And the siren's songs*
> *I conjure you*
> *To cease your anger*

And not touch the wall,
That the bride may sleep in deeper peace.

This is after all the origin of art - verbalizing that which is beyond words. Art is the effort to express by symbols and images that which is beyond our conceptual ideas and our limited senses. As he himself says at the beginning of the Spiritual Canticle: *this is why through images, verses and comparisons these beloved souls allow some of what they feel to be expressed ...*

A breeze of poetry

The critic Menendez y Pelayo when commenting on the poetry of Saint John of the Cross wrote in these terms: *Although here we are faced with an evangelical poetry, which is both heavenly and divine, so much so that one gets the feeling that it does not belong to this earth, and hence it is difficult to analyse it with the normal literary criteria, this poetry is at the same time aflame with a more intense passion than any other profane poetry. It is so eloquent and deliciously formed, as plastic and figurative as the most sublime fruit of the Renaissance. I confess that these verses fill me with a religious awe when I handle them. Here the Spirit of God has passed, embellishing and sanctifying everything.*

In a way this critique surprises us, as many are surprised when they first come face to face with the literary output of this poet, expecting to find whole volumes of poetry ready to assail them. The truth is that Saint John of the Cross wrote very little. There is an impressive disproportion between the limited quantity of his writings and the outstanding fame he achieved. He wrote only twenty poems - 956 verses in all. Indeed the three poems by which he acquired his renown, namely the **Spiritual Canticle** (40 stanzas, 200 verses), the **Dark Night** (8 stanzas, 40 verses) and the **Living Flame of Love** (4 stanzas, 24 verses) contain only 264 verses in all.

Writing was never that important to him. He is not a writer by profession. His community life with the friars, the administration of monasteries, the spiritual formation of his disciples and manual work in the monastery were much more urgent to him. He wrote his poems in moments of crisis and the commentaries on the poems when and if he found the time.

His first poetic creation is the **Spiritual Canticle**. He wrote it at the age of 35 when he was in prison in Toledo. Since for nine whole months he could speak to no one, he gave vent to his feelings in song. To give vent to one's feelings one does not need a public; two persons are enough - himself and God. The Spiritual Canticle is considered the apex of Spanish lyricism. It is a forceful poem, full of emotion:

> *Where have you hidden Beloved,*
> *and left me moaning?*
> *You fled like a stag*
> *after wounding me;*
> *I went out calling You,*
> *and You were gone.*

Later, touched by an experience of profound intimacy with God which few have ever achieved, Saint John of the Cross wrote the **Living Flame of Love**, a poem and commentary which leaves anyone who reads them stunned. He wrote them at the insistence of a lady, Doña Ana del Mercado y Penalosa.

John believed that man was created for excellence. His raison d'etre is to enjoy full and intimate union with God. He uses a powerful biblical word: God's desire is to *marry* man. Hence everything becomes fire, a living fire of love. *Love is never static, but it is always dynamic, like a flame from which tongues of fire issue in all directions.*

> *O living flame of love*
> *That tenderly wounds my soul*
> *In its deepest centre*
> *Since now you are not oppressive*
> *now consummate if it be Your will:*
> *Tear through the veil of this sweet encounter.*
>
> *O sweet cautery; O delightful wound*
> *O gentle hand; O delicate touch*
> *that tastes of eternal life*
> *and pays every debt*
> *In killing You changed death to life.*

But Saint John of the Cross' name remained ever linked with the other two short books which he wrote as a partial commentary on the poem **The Dark Night**. The symbolism of the Night has caught the imagination of many.

One dark night,
fired with love's urgent longings
Ah, the sheer grace!
I went out unseen,
my house being now all stilled; ...
This light guided me more surely
than the light of noon
to where He waited for me
Him I knew so well
in a place where no one else appeared.

His poems have a mystical quality and a transcendental literary character very difficult to find in any other writing.

The rest of his works were written in Andalucia when he was 42 - 45 years old. Today the two other poems which are relished by many are **La Fuente** *(Que bien se yo la fuente ......!)* and the romance Sobre la Trinidad y la Encarnacion because of the richness of their symbolic and biblical content.   In the last four years of his life he wrote nothing.

Notwithstanding this limited literary output, on the 21st March 1952 the poets of Spain acclaimed him as their patron. Damaso Alonso, when commenting on the last stanzas of the Spiritual Canticle acknowledges: *On other occasions we have doubted; is this man a natural poet or a reckless technician? Here we can no longer doubt; he who wrote this poem, he who could develop such a lengthy theme with such ardour and such elegance, with classical perfection and such fiery spirit, must surely be a perfect artist.* Professor E. Allison Peers, who for many years was considered the greatest expert on the Saint in the English language, in his book **Spirit of Flame,** even calls him *the poet's poet.*

John lived in an era when the fortunes of Spain were in the ascendant. The Golden Age of Castille... The time of Philip II... The decade when the Escorial was being built. This is the period of the great European expansion: Spain and Portugal are discovering America, the Portuguese have reached Canton in China. El Greco leads the field of painting while Garciloso de la Vega, Luis de Leon and Cervantes dominate the world of literature.

This is the supreme apex of the Italian Renaissance: Machiavelli, Tiziano, Michelangelo, Leonardo da Vinci, Raffaello, Tintoretto, Cellini, Pier Luigi da Palestrina. In England, we find William Shakespeare. Man's imagination is bursting. This is the age of Copernicus. A new world.

There is a spirit of reform abroad the Church. This is the age of the Council of Trent, the season of Saint Ignatius of Loyola, Saint Teresa, Saint Philip Neri. A time of challenges, risks and divisions. Grim ruptures in the structure of the church, internal and external conflicts - Luther, Calvin, the Spanish Inquisition, the tragedy of the Huguenots. It is the time of the apogee of the Knights of Malta. As Pope John Paul II said in the Apostolic Exhortation *Maestro en la fe* - which he issued on the occasion of the fourth centenary of the death of Saint John of the Cross - this is a world which is very similar to the world we live in today. [4]

The Secret

The genius of John of the Cross reflected in his poetry all these characteristics of his age. But he was able to develop these features in a new trail-blazing dimension which goes far beyond human history because it enters the realm of eternity. He is a creative person, very original. He encompasses everything in his contemplative vocation knowing that only God can possibly unify and give meaning to all this varied reality.

For him, all human endeavour - theology, philosophy, psychology, humanism - is art. Everything can become a song because everything reminds him of God. It is enough to look around to be overwhelmed by the *hermosura* - the beauty and radiance of creation, man, history. Faced with all this, the only plausible reaction is to raise his eyes and heart to this God who cares so deeply for man:

> *Let us rejoice, Beloved,*
> *and let us go forth*
> *to behold ourselves in Your beauty,*
> *To the mountain and to the hill,*
> *to where the pure water flows,*
> *and further, deep into the thicket.*

And in his commentary on the verse *And let us go forth to behold ourselves in your beauty,* he explodes into the ecstatic delirium of an artist who is in euphoria in front of this Beauty with a capital B: *This means: Let us so act that by means of this loving activity we may attain to the vision of ourselves in Your* Beauty *in eternal life. That is: that I be so transformed in your* Beauty *that we may be alike in* Beauty, *and both behold ourselves in your* Beauty, *possessing now your very* Beauty; *this, in such a way that each looking at the other may see in the other his own* Beauty, *since both are your* Beauty *alone, I being absorbed in your* Beauty; *hence I shall see you in your* Beauty, *and I shall see myself in you in your* Beauty, *and you will see yourself in me in your* Beauty; *that I may resemble you in your* Beauty, *and you resemble me in your* Beauty, *and my* Beauty *be your* Beauty *and your* Beauty *my* Beauty; *wherefore I shall be you in your* Beauty, *and you will be me in your* Beauty, *because your very* Beauty *will be my* Beauty; *and therefore we shall behold each other in your* Beauty. Hermosura indeed!!

This is the key to understand this man. Saint John of the Cross is a mystic. He is a man of God. Pope John Paul II, a real enthusiast of Saint John of the Cross (*I myself,* he avows, *felt drawn by the experiences and teaching of the Saint of Fontiveros,* calls him a *romantic lover of God.* In his apostolic letter **Master of Faith** he states: *Saint John of the Cross had fallen deeply in love with God. He had great familiarity with God and always spoke to him and of him. God was in his heart and on his lips, because God was his true treasure, his true world. Before proclaiming and singing the mystery of God, he was a witness of God; he used to speak of God with a fervour and conviction which were remarkably exceptional.*

When one is imbued with God, everything around him becomes God. His artistic prowess flowers into infinity! There has never been a mystic who, as Saint John of the Cross was able to join the highest artistic intuition with the highest contemplation. For this reason his poems emerge like the breath of God in the language of men. The boy of Fontiveros, the exile of Penuela, the prisoner of Toledo has experienced with the incomparable intensity of a lover, the beauty of nature, which is nothing else but the reflection of the beauty of God. In his spiritual Canticle, while we see the hidden valleys filled with trees and the mountains open up before our eyes, we find in them not only a physical freshness which enthrals us, but something else too - the holiness of the poet, a vitality which encourages us to prayer and leads us to God. The glory of poetry lies in the fact that it is the expression of man which can border the divine mystery. No poetry stimulates us to contemplate God more than the poetry of John...[5]

Saint John of the Cross himself describes his works thus: *Contar y cantar las grandezas de su Amado - in these stanzas the soul does nothing more than recount and sing of the great deeds of her Beloved!!* (Canticle 14) *The will is enkindled in loving, desiring, praising and thanking God, and reverencing, esteeming, and praying to Him in the savour of love* (Canticle 25). In this same Spiritual Canticle we come across phrases which are riveting: *The strength of the soul lies in loving God. Everything works in love and through love. In the end, it was for this love that we were created. The heart can be satisfied by nothing but God. The aim of everything is love.*

Here we have a man who entered into an adventure without limits, and discovered that God is not an abstract idea with no practical gist in life, but that he is *el todo, the all,* as he used to enjoy calling Him.

> *My Beloved is the mountains,*
> *and lonely wooded valleys,*
> *strange islands,*
> *and resounding rivers,*
> *the whistling of love-stirring breezes,*
> *the tranquil night at the time of the rising dawn,*
> *silent music,*
> *sounding solitude,*
> *the supper that refreshes, and deepens love.*

This... and more is God for Saint John of the Cross; and so he focused his life on Him. He concentrated all his life on God because he felt himself totally loved by Him. John called God *el principal amante, el amado* - the bridegroom who is always searching out new ways to be close to his bride. Once the bride finds herself wounded by this sweet and unconditional love, her life becomes a continual tension in an effort to know him better and to love him more, so that she might harmonize herself perfectly with him.

This is the basis of his artistic creation. If one were to separate his experience of God from his poetry, all his artistic calibre would dissolve. The beauty, the quintessence, the love of God are the poetic heart of Saint John of the Cross.

An enterprising life

Let us be clear. We are not talking about a man who lived in a world of fantasy. Today we appreciate him as a mystic and a poet, but he lived out these values in a busy life. Early in life he experienced pain and suffering. When he was two, his older brother died. When he was eight he lost his father and when he was twelve his mother sent him to an orphanage for poor children. At the age of fifteen he began to work in a hospital for infectious diseases. At the age of twenty-one he joined the Carmelite Order. At the age of twenty four, still a newly ordained priest, he underwent a serious vocational crisis. He met Saint Teresa who persuaded him to start a reform in his own Carmelite Order. At the age of thirty five, he suffered imprisonment - nine months on a diet of bread, water and sardines. At the age of forty seven, his own colleagues turned their back on him and he had to taste the bitterness of injustice. But this suffering did not make him cynical. On the contrary, it led him to enter deeply the mystery of human existence. He experienced that dark night which he described so well in his writings:

> *O night that has united*
> *the lover with his beloved,*
> *transforming the beloved in her lover.* [6]

All this moulded his character. An independent character, he was careful not to lose his precious energy in peripherals. He kept non-essential things at a distance not for mortification sake, but because superfluous things kept him from his aim in life. He was a pensive, dignified person, rather reserved but at the same time jovial. He enjoyed making others happy. Still waters ran deep. His writings are all the result of long years of maturing both of his own personal interior experience as well as of his oral teaching. This interior experience flowered first into poetry and later in his doctrinal commentaries. In his writings we have the two faces of the soul of Saint John of the Cross: song and passion on the one hand, reflection and analysis on the other.

He was a very dynamic man. It is calculated that he travelled more than 26,000 kilometres during his lifetime (and at that time travelling was not at all comfortable); but throughout his activity he was able to keep a serene and contemplative depth. He was very sensitive in his relationships with men and with nature. Very tender in his relationship with God.

The sacristan of the Granada monastery tells us: *He used to be very grateful to whoever brought a rose or a carnation to honour the Blessed Sacrament.* He loved sculpture, painting and music. All his poems are hymns, songs of joy, of sorrow, of hope, most of all of love and praise. This is how his earliest disciples read them and sang them. Saint Teresa used to enjoy singing his most renowned poem *Adonde te escondiste?* and she herself taught her nuns a melody so that they could sing it frequently in the community. It is a shame that tape-recorders had not been invented!!

Towards the ineffable

In his writings, his basic problem is always the same: how can one express God? Man can only stammer, *un no sè que. Lord you love discretion, you love light, most of all you love love. Hence these will be sayings of discretion for the wayfarer, of light for the way, and of love in the wayfaring. May there be nothing of worldly rhetoric in them nor the long winded and dry eloquence of weak and artificial human wisdom* - thus he begins the *Dichos de luz y amor.* [7] *It is impossible to say what God communicates to the soul in this intimate union. One can say nothing, in the same way as one can say nothing which truly resembles what God is in Himself, because He gives Himself to the soul achieving a glorious transformation of the soul into Himself*, he declares in the Spiritual Canticle. When once John asked a brother, Fray Francesco, who God was to him, the brother answered *For me, God is what he wishes to be.* This answer so pleased him that he kept repeating it for a long time.

God is transcendent. This however does not leave John breathless; on the contrary it fills him with courage! The mystery fascinates him because it puts his life in tension. And the only way by which he can express this experience is poetry where he can use the art of symbolism to the full. Symbols can express better the sentiments of the heart: emotions, tenderness, romance, moods... What makes his poetry so beautiful is the musicality of his verse, the lack of the hyperbole and exaggeration which was so typical of his time, his elegant technique, but most of all the depth of the images he uses. When Sister Magdalene asked him in her simplicity *Whether it was God himself who had given him these fine words,* he answered, half evasively but also sincerely, *Sometimes God gave me these words, sometimes I sought for them myself.*

He uses two basic symbols: marriage and night. Both of them have a long history both within and outside the Christian tradition. The night today has a stronger resonance in the contemporary society and many feel tuned with this poet specifically because of the realistic way in which he described the night. However there is a tendency to abuse this image. For him "the night" is not mreely suffering - which happens to us all - but the attitude one should adopt when confronted by pain and its interpretation in the light of faith and hope so that we can find in it the love of God.

Once his works had been written, they take on a life of their own -they become independent of him. They are now children who are no longer tied to their parent. John of the Cross emphasizes this. In the commentary which he wrote both for the **Spiritual Canticle** and for the **Living Flame** he says: *It is best that the word of love should be allowed space so that each person may receive benefit from it according to the nature and size of his soul. This is far better than trying to insist on the same interpretation for all people.* Poetry is but a portrait that has a value and an existence because of what it is and of what it represents not because of its writer. Thus we can all freely roam around the garden of his poetry. We do not have to feel tied down to any predetermined scheme of things. Man is free when he is tasting God.

Manuel Machado exclaims: *Oh greatest poet among all the saints ... and most saintly among all the poets!!* The Pope adds *The example of his life is an ideal of life, his writings are treasures which should be shared with all those who are seeking the face of God, his doctrine is a relevant word for today.* Before us we have a whole voyage of discovery ...

His poetry brings us into contact with the passion of his life and furnishes us with an enormous space for personal creativity. I hope that many will have the opportunity *to live* the same passionate poetry of Saint John of the Cross and *to meet* this *Love which sings*, which is none other than God Himself.

□

His Life

We cannot understand someone
unless we know how he lived.
It is the experience which builds
or breaks a man.

Juan de la Cruz is an interesting person
because he is one of the few persons
who lived out what he believed.
He discovered Love and lived for It.
For It alone.

He was not the kind of person who enjoyed
talking about himself
And so we know very little about him.
However we know enough to appreciate
and long for the same adventure
that he lived with God.

It is a life that can fill us with hope.
We too can encounter this Love and share this joy
and behold ourselves in his beauty
and go further, deep into the thicket...

Always further. Always deeper.

O sweet cautery, O delightful wound [8]

We do not know either the day nor the month when
he was born. We only know the year: 1542. Juan de Yepes
Alvarez was born in Fontiveros, a village near Avila. Dry
in summer, cold and arid in winter. His parents' marriage
was a poem of love. Gonzalo de Yepes, coming from a
rich family of Toledo fell in love with Catalina Alvarez - a
beautiful girl endowed with many human traits but not a
penny to call her own. His family opposed vigorously a
marriage which would degrade their son to a lower social
class. They threatened to disinherit him. He felt that love
is more important than money and he did not heed their
threats. Gonzalo married Catalina and became penniless.
Thus, this young man who had been used to the cozy life of
a gentleman, suddenly found himself in a situation where
he had to fend for himself. He learnt the art of weaving
silk, which was his wife's trade. It was hard work which
did not pay well. Indeed, for some time they even had to
struggle against hunger.

They had three sons: Francisco (1530), Luis (date of
birth unknown) and Juan. When John was six, his father
became very ill. He was bed ridden for two years thus
using up all the family's savings. His death meant that life
became much harder for the de Yepes family. The familiar
situation was made worse by a famine which affected the
whole of Castille.

Catalina decided to seek assistance from the family
of her husband. She left Fontiveros and went to Toledo.
John was still a baby. However all doors were closed to

this poor widow. From Toledo she went to Galvez where her husband's brother lived. This man, a doctor who had no children, decided to take Francisco under his care. However, his wife made life so difficult for Francisco that the boy soon had to return to his mother. Meanwhile, Catalina had returned to Fontiveros. There Luis died. From a family of five, in a few months they had been reduced to a family of three. The shock of two bereavements, so close to each other, left their mark on young Juan.

Life was very hard at Fontiveros, so Catalina decided to emigrate to Arevalo. This was a difficult decision since it meant leaving the place where she had her most beautiful memories. The situation did not improve and after three years she had to load all her possessions on a donkey and travel again, this time to Medina del Campo - a city of 30,000 inhabitants where there was more trade. Within the space of 12 years, Juan had already lived in four different places. The poor rarely find openings in life, and even in Medina, the family's position did not improve.

This poverty left a deep mark on the sensitive character of the boy. God did not intend his genius to be wasted in the normal bustle of everyday work. The family never made a tragedy out of their poverty. Indeed, both at Arevalo and at Medina, his mother would often gather together some poor children, take them home, share what little food the family had with them. Early in life Juan learnt that *love is a flame which burns with a wish to burn more fiercely...* Christian optimism always finds room in the poor heart that knows how to look ahead. During this time an unusual incident took place. While he was playing,

Juan fell into a deep pool. He panicked and was going to drown when *he saw a beautiful woman who held out her hand so that he could hold it. He did not wish to take her hand so as not to smear it.* A farmer arrived and saved him. *The Mother of God, is all mine,* he would say later.

Juan spent his youth in Medina - a time of dreams, a time of enthusiasm, a time of hope. In this city, his mother enroled him in an orphanage for small children, the College of Doctrine. An intelligent solution because here children were given food and clothes and taught the first elements of reading and writing. Being still young, he loved serving the priest as an altar boy, and he spent hours on end in the church of the Magdalene. He even acted as godparent in some baptisms!

Meanwhile, his teachers tried to coach him into a trade. He tried his hand as carpenter, painter, tailor, sculptor. All in vain! He was not the practical type! His brother Francis later said: *He did not manage to learn a trade although he loved to work.* Later, however, this apprenticeship would help him. God never does anything for nothing.

From the College he moved to the hospital of the Conception. The man in charge there had probably noticed him because of his serious bearing. Now he was to take care of the sick. He enjoyed this work. So much so, that even later when he began his higher studies, he did not desert it. As well as caring for the sick, he was also charged with going from house to house begging charity to fund the hospital. The director of the hospital, Don Alonso

Alvarez de Toledo, was very impressed by him. Therefore, he was entrusted with more and more weighty work. His childhood, with all its privations, had infused in his blood a love for those who suffer. The poor assess the needs of others immediately.

He was not good at trades but books fascinated him. He read and studied more and more. He used every free minute from his hospital work to pour over his books. He often stayed up reading late at night. The hospital director encouraged him ... especially as he planned that one day John might become the hospital chaplain.

Growing up, Juan started discovering himself. He was now seventeen. He began following the regular art course at the recently opened Jesuit college. Here he found enough material to stimulate his interest: Latin literature, the Greek classics and contemporary Spanish writers. He was interested in all that could broaden his mind. He learnt to write with intensity, poetic finesse and logic. He liked poetry. He was a teenager who could recognize the vastness and the fine detail of creation about him.

I want to spend my time only in love...

He spent five years studying and helping in the hospital. This was the time when he began to consider what to do with his life. He felt God was drawing him strongly to Himself. He began to understand that *Love can only be repaid with love.* He could join the Jesuits whom he knew well. He could stay in the hospital and become the chaplain there as his protector wished. In this way he could also improve his family's financial position, which had never recovered from its poverty. He decided to become a Carmelite. An unexpected decision. This was his first major choice - to leave his books and the world and become a friar in the Monastery of Our Lady of Carmel in Medina. Two motives determined this choice: his ardent desire for solitude in which to pray and his devotion to the Virgin of Nazareth. These two motives, had been ingrained in his character since he was young. *The soul should seek not what is most easy but that which is most difficult* ... not because it feels constrained to, but because it is drawn by Love. — God.

We know nothing of his one-year long novitiate. He was given the name John of Saint Mattias. A year of novitiate means practically a year alone where one is moulded into the new life through reading, devotions, community acts, and the vigilant eye of the Novice Master. Carmel could offer him a very abundant and stimulating ascetic and historical tradition. He could let his eager spirit roam freely in the fresh air of Carmel. This was a year when his relationship with God could mature.

Having finished his novitiate successfully, his Superiors sent him to Salamanca to study philosophy and theology. He was 22. He moved from literature to philosophy. His Order owned in Salamanca the inter-provincial college of Saint Andrew; here students from all over Spain could come together to continue their spiritual and intellectual formation... They used to attend the courses in the university. He spent four decisive years here. They were decisive because they again sparked off tension within his ever-searching soul.

Salamanca is a university city. At that time it could compete with the universities of Oxford and Paris. The best professors were there... Soto, Melchior Cano, fra Luis de Leon, Hugo de San Victor. All subjects were studied. It was a town full of young people. However, Salamanca confused him. Although it offered the best professors, books, scholastic environment and students ... he soon realized that he had not become a friar to build a career for himself. He had become a friar to find God. His studies were useful only if they helped him find God. He began to feel that the ideal to which he had committed himself was slipping through his fingers and he did not wish to waste his life. *Who seeks for nothing but God does not walk in darkness, even if he perceives himself to be poor and in darkness.*

Therefore he tries to go deeper in his studies. He analyzes more closely Scripture, he studies the Fathers of the Church (Saint Dionysus and Saint Gregory were his favorites because of their mysticism full of ardor and love), he goes deeper into Theology. In the College of the Order the Superiors appoint him as prefect of the students - a sign that his results were good. Occasionally the prefect was supposed to give lessons and to answer the student's difficulties. Naturally his innate spirit of recollection gave him the necessary mental space to be able to go deep into things. His insights were deep and alert.

His colleagues recognized his virtues - something which is not very common in monasteries! It is easier to notice the defects of others than to recognize their qualities. Original sin exists even in monasteries! Brother John continued on his way. Without any noise or outward show, he fasted frequently, he wore a hair shirt, he preferred a poor dark room... but when the occasion offered itself, he immediately changed his room for another one from where he could see the tabernacle in the Church. The wise know how to choose. Here he could learn another science: intimacy with God.

His closeness to God increased, rather than reduced his inner tension. *Who can understand the Lord?* asks the Psalmist. Our God is a God who never allows man to stand still. And in order to move him forward He always places man in a crisis. From crisis to crisis God leads us on toward himself. Later on, John would refer to the road towards God as *Night.* Radicality is basic to Christianity. This young man of twenty five took God and himself seriously to such an extent that he put at risk even the most personal values of his life.

As time went on, he realized more and more that despite all his good will, he could not mature in this kind of religious life organized as a social profession for cultured and educated people but with a very poor religious content. He felt that he could not settle to any compromises since here there was his life at stake. *What profiteth the man if he gain all the world and then ....*

He began speculating whether to leave Carmel and join the Carthusians. They would offer him - he thought - a suitable environment where he could belong only to his

Beloved. But he was afraid. He did not want to make another mistake. He knows where he wants to go but he does not know how to get there. He is not the dynamic type. He is rather timid and reserved. God ALWAYS chooses the weak. Moses stuttered, David was a sinner, Jeremiah a coward...

One dark night ... I went out unseen ...

While he was going through this interior night, he was ordained a priest. In the summer of 1567, together with Brother Pedro de Orozco, he returns to Medina to sing his first Solemn Mass. His mother and his brother Francis live there and they are overjoyed to see their son and brother celebrating the Eucharist.

God meanwhile is building something new. By one of his divine random coincidences, at that time in Medina there was Mother Teresa of Jesus, who had just left the convent of San Jose, Avila after five years, to found her second monastery of Discalced nuns. She was already 52 years old. She had also permission to found a monastery of friars so that they too could live the reform she wanted to introduce into Carmel. She had already found one friar - the prior of the Toledo monastery - Padre Antonio. However, she was rather uncertain about him because, although he was a *recollected, studious friar, loving his cell and wise,* he was sixty years old, he was *too sickly* and loved his appearance too much! Women have a deep insight into human nature.

'By chance', Fra Pedro, Brother John's companion, went to speak to Mother Teresa and told her about this young 25 year-old friar full of zeal and prayer. She sent for him. They met only once but this was enough for Teresa: *When I spoke to him I was very pleased with him.* She called him *my little Seneca.* She suggested the Reformed Carmel to him. She did not give him his vocation - she found him well-suited, cut out for the style of life which she had in mind. John had already been thinking on similar lines. However it was she who gave a concrete orientation to his thoughts and hopes. Indeed, being the woman she was, she offered him another strong argument to entice him to her project: he could achieve all that he wished for without leaving his religious family, a Marian and contemplative family. He accepted. Now he had a definite project before his eyes, a serious way to fulfill his longings. He made only one condition: *that she should not take too long.* People who love God are always impatient with the things of God. He returned to Salamanca happy because he had again discovered the faithfulness of God. *God is like a sun which shines on souls in order to give himself to them.* For the moment he kept silent about this project.

The following summer (1568), he is available to embark on this new venture because he has finished his studies. Above all, he was prepared in his heart, because maybe without him even realizing it, God had chosen him for a mission of great creativity. Mother Teresa therefore invited him to accompany her to the foundation of her monastery in Vallidolid. In this way this young man could see with his own eyes and touch with his own hands the spirit that Teresa was developing in the new life of Carmel. This direct contact with the Mother Superior and the nuns helped him a great deal. *Since humble people never think of pretending to be teachers, they are ready to move forward and take a different route from that which they are already in, if they are ordered by someone to do so, because they never expect to achieve anything.* John allowed this woman to lead him and form him in this new charism.

She in turn confirmed her high opinion of him. She wrote enthusiastically: *Father John is one of the purest and holiest souls that God has in his Church: God had put a great treasure of heavenly wisdom in his heart.* Often they do not agree and many a time she pulls his leg: *God deliver us from those who turn everything into a high degree of contemplation. It is impossible to talk to brother John, because he goes at once into an ecstasy and draws you in with him!* She just loves him.

Meanwhile Mother Teresa had found a small house where they can create *the little Bethlehem* of the Reformed Carmel for men. Don Rafael Mejia offered her a farmhouse in Duruelo: a small entrance, a room divided into two, a loft, a small kitchen ... that is all! More of a shack than a building. When Sister Antonia saw the place, she told Mother Teresa: *no man, good though he may be, will be capable of living here.* Father John and Father Antonio insist that they will live even in a pig-sty!!

So Father John went at once to the farmhouse to begin working on it. He had already put on the new habit which Mother Teresa herself had modeled. A new life, a new spirit, a new habit. Prayer, manual work, catechesis is the nearby villages... this was their life. It was a simple life but he was so happy. They ate the bread which the farmers nearby gave them. They filled the place with crosses and skulls. They were so excited... they ate the daily ration of bread *with greater enjoy ment than if they had been eating partridge.*

Slowly he was learning how true it is that the will of God is a delicious bread which fills and satisfies us. The experiences of the beginning are always the most beautiful.

On 27th November 1568 Father Alonso Gonzalez, the provincial, arrived at Duruelo. He was an *elderly (priest), holy and very good.* He arrived with five other Carmelite friars to inaugurate this new initiative. The event was so emotion-filled that the provincial started crying with joy when he saw the place. Father Antonio complained because another friar had put on the new habit before him... The next day, the first Sunday of Advent, the provincial said a Mass during which Brother Antonio de Heredia, Brother Juan de San Mattia and the deacon Brother Joseph of Christ professed that they would live according to the primitive rule of Carmel. [9]

Father John, who is now twenty six, changes his surname. When he joined the Carmelite Order, his family name *de Yepes* was changed to *de San Mattia.* Instead he now chooses a new surname which means a whole new programme: *of the Cross.* Here he was born, on it he wants to live. Like his Master. For the Christian, the cross is not a stupidity, nor a scandal, nor does it mean resignation. It is an enormous gift of God, his Father, through which he will discover the glorious face of God. *On the contrary embrace the cross, and crucified on it*

Answer?

+ Deny Self -

36

drink vinegar and sweet bitterness and consider this a great fortune, because you will see how, while you thus die to the world and to yourselves, you will live in God with the joy of the Spirit.

They rapidly organize their lives. When a few months later Saint Teresa visited them, she was so happy: *I arrived in the morning and Father Antonio was sweeping the threshold of the chapel with that typical smile of his. I told him what am I seeing here? ! Where have all your honours gone? ! I curse the time when I had any! he answered me while he began to tell me of the great joy he had ... There were so many crosses and so many skulls!! ... I heard that after matins, instead of going out, they would stay there praying until Prime, and their prayer was so fervent and so deep that sometimes, when they would rise, they would find their clothes covered with snow which had fallen without their even noticing!!*

An exaggeration? No, This is common sense. Evangelical common sense. When one finds a treasure, he sells everything in order to acquire it. And he does it willingly and joyfully. *They used to preach in the small villages nearby where the people had no religious teaching ... The joy they felt made everything easy for them.* They insisted that they should not be reckless and weaken themselves with too much penance. They ... did not pay much heed to her recommendations! *It is like when an artist wishes to paint a face. If the model moves, he prevents the artist from doing his work properly. In the same way here; every activity the soul may make here confuses her and confounds her.* There is a time when one must remain still and quiet before God. And penance helps to keep one still, thus allowing God to shape that person in His own image. The sacrifices which John is doing arise spontaneously from this interior deepness.

God does not destroy the pleasures of life. He intensifies them. In the night one discovers God on a much deeper level. As the fire first dries the humidity of the wood, then darkens it, then warms it, and at last changes it into itself and makes it transparent and red, so the divine fire of contemplative love transforms the soul. The Christian knows that there is a road always open in front of him.

From this spring and from these waters comes forth a torrent...

Some months later, the provincial, pleased with how matters are going, makes the foundation a priory, with the faculty of receiving novices. Indeed soon, young men started coming. The Gospel attracts people, for when its message becomes flesh in simple people, it becomes contagious. So Duruelo soon became too small, and a year and a half later they leave it to go to Mancera, just one mile from Duruelo.

Meanwhile Mother Teresa had founded another friar's monastery at Pastrana, and, since some young men from the nearby university of Alcalà de Henares were interested in joining this new evangelical life, Mother Teresa felt that Father John should go there to form them in the rigorous yet vibrant Teresian spirit. So in 1570 he moved from Mancera to Pastrana. Here start his voyages, always on foot, barefoot, with no money in his pocket. The gospel is not an utopia. In this monastery he finds five religious priests coming from different orders and ten novices. He organizes life along the lines that they had led in Duruelo and Mancera. His intuition as a formator was simple: *he who has fallen in love knows how to separate himself at once from all else in order to acquire what he loves.* He offers them a chance to live a true experience of the love of God and then everything will follow naturally. It is not a question of loathing things but a question of loving God and yourself and then choosing what is most befitting.

He did not stay long in Pastrana because after only one month he had to go and help Mother Teresa in the founding of the nun's convent in Alba de Tormes. Here he co-operates with the builders in the building of the house, and with the nuns in the building of the living temple of their bodies.

From Alba he goes to Alcalà de Henares, where a college of studies for the Discalced had just been founded. Every responsibility which had to do with formation was entrusted to him. And so he finds himself rector of the college. He would never again see Duruelo ... His motto with the young students was *a religious and a student; but first a religious.* Alcalà was a beautiful experience for him. Convinced of *the twelve stars which lead to God, namely love of God, love of neighbor, obedience, poverty, chastity, presence in choir, penance, humility, mortification, prayer, quiet, peace,* he worked hard to be of service to the students that the Lord had put into his life. He was straightforward and earnest in his approach but at the same time he knew how to be humane and affable. He even had to go to Pastrana for some weeks to restrain the sterile ardor of the master of novices who had been multiplying mortifications and penances. *Some get angry with their imperfections and show a lack of patience which is against humility. They are so impatient that they want to become saints in a day!!* And these people tend to coerce others to sanctity!!

In 1572 he had to move again. This time he finds himself in Avila as the spiritual director of the convent of the Incarnation. Mother Teresa had in fact been ordered by the Apostolic Visitor to take over the leadership of the convent of nuns from where she had left to begin her reform. At once she realized the necessity of having a firm and confident hand to support her. Therefore she asked and received permission for Father John to come as one of the spiritual directors of the nuns. It was a wise move, since although still very young (30 years of age), he was very mature spiritually, to such an extent that he began to direct qualified people like Saint Teresa. It was at that time that she reached the peak of her mystical experiences - the spiritual marriage (1572). He was able to eliminate slowly many abuses which had filtered into the convent life, and he did this with such dexterity that soon practically all the nuns were frequenting him for confession. Since trouble was again brewing between the Calced and the Discalced, Mother Teresa invited Father John to leave the Calced monastery and together with another friar, come and live in a small house just outside the nun's garden.

He wished to live a quiet life, but ... On one occasion

a beautiful noble girl fell madly in love with him. One night she even climbed over the garden wall to find him alone in his house. He was eating and was amazed when he saw her there. He did not become angry with her. He spoke kindly to her and she burst into tears and returned home. On another occasion a knight, who was angry because the nun with whom he was having an illicit relationship, left him as soon as she began to go to confession to Father John, ambushed him and gave him a good beating. *I felt the blows as sweet as the stones they threw at Saint Stephen.* Powerful man indeed, but only through the strength of God. Another young rich girl, beautiful but haughty, was persuaded, much against her will, to go to confession to him. She was terrorized because she was afraid he would reproach her. *You think I am a saint,* he told her, *I am not. But know that the more saintly a confessor is, the kinder he is and the less is he scandalized by the sins of others because he knows well the situation of man.* How true this is!

The atmosphere of the monastery began to change. Zeal increased. Joy increased. Prayer increased. Community Spirit increased. The sisters always remembered the little notes he used to pass to them on which he wrote short forceful remarks which reminded them of his teaching. *He always filled us with courage* they stated later. He did not base his teaching on fear and punishment but on loving and caring. God is rich in mercy. They always remembered the nights he would spend awake with the sick nuns. He would do all he could to help the poor nuns who lived in the convent - once he even went out to beg money from his friends to buy sandals for a nun who did not have any. The nuns say that his prayer was so strong that he often cured them of illness. All is possible for those who believe.

Even Mother Teresa was impressed. *I believe it was Father John who brought about all this change in the convent. He used to look after the hearts and the souls of the nuns.* Everything rested on hope and on his conviction that God loves sinners. He would speak a great deal of the presence of God.

In his small room near the convent he used also to teach catechism and from time to time reading skills to children. Sometimes he painted. In Avila they still treasure a card on which he drew the crucified Jesus after having a vision. Saint Teresa was very pleased with him: *after he left I could find no one like him in the whole of Castille!* she was to remark later.

O guiding night, night that I loved you...

He did not leave Avila. He was abducted! For a long time dark heavy clouds have been gathering over the Calced and the Discalced. Far too many mistakes had been made on both sides. And so suspicions, mistrust and scepticism grew and grew. We know well enough who sows the tares among the wheat! Finally the storm erupted. The Chapter General of Piacenza (1575), following the one sided information that they had received, decided that this Discalced experiment in Spain must end. No further houses should be opened. Those monasteries which had been founded without the permission of Father General were to close. Mother Teresa was to return to the enclosure in a convent of her choice. The Discalced friars were all to be absorbed into Calced monasteries. The Chapter felt it necessary also to order that, where necessary, the Fathers should ask for the help of the local civil authorities to enforce these directives. The lack of diplomacy of some and the envy of others brought about this war between brothers. The Discalced found themselves in a dilemma, because on the one hand they had received a clear order coming from the Chapter and on the other the Papal Legate in Spain demanded that they should continue. Who were they to obey?

In September 1576, Father Gracian, nominated superior of the Discalced by the Legate, called a chapter at Almadovar del Campo to which were invited the nine superiors of the monasteries of the reform. Father John was specifically invited because he was the first Discalced friar. To complicate things more, an internal problem arose. Should the friars limit their pastoral work? Some insisted on the contemplative life, others on the pastoral life. Many elements which were foreign to the charism had already entered the Discalced Carmel because many friars had entered the Order with an entrenched mentality which was alien to the innovative spirit of this new religious family. They believed too much in the law. Father John, convinced that *if the soul seeks God, God also is seeking it,* and that the greatest apostolate is that *the soul should be happy with God alone* insisted on the contemplative element of the charism.

Meanwhile it was suggested that it would be better for him not to remain confessor of the nuns at Avila to avoid further trouble. A few months before, Father Valdemoro, the prior of the Calced, had seized Father John violently from his home and detained him in the monastery for some time.

This was only a prelude to what was to happen on the 2nd December 1577. While Father John was asleep with his companion, a group of Calced Carmelite friars arrived, broke down the door, captured Father John and his companion, tied them up and took them to the monastery. When they told Father John that they had come to arrest him, his answer was simple: *Good! Let us go!* Following the customs of the time, they smote him twice, stripped him of his Discalced habit and gave him that of a Calced friar, and a few days later, *although weakened because of much suffering* (Saint Teresa), they took him to the monastery of Toledo. Mother Teresa wrote with great concern to King Philip II: *I would prefer him to be in the hands of the Moors than in their hands* !

Their intention was good: convert him from the mistake they believed him to be in. Their method was however questionable and disproportionate. Father John found himself in a small dark room living on a regime of water, bread and sardines. This was a painful experience - a small, humid room, cold in winter, hot in summer, practically no light, a hard bed and the impossibility of ever changing his clothes. He was kept in solitary confinement except when his guard, who showed him little or no sympathy, brought him food. Three times a week, following the Constitutions, they would bring him to the refectory and there deliver the blows of the discipline (a small rope whip) on his shoulders. He underwent a major crisis, wondering whether it made sense to continue following his principles - listening today, listening tomorrow about his lack of obedience, about his obstinacy ... he begins to wonder whether after all he had been completely off track. A very dark crisis, especially when one considers that at the time, everything was going wrong for the Discalced. *God now chooses to strip the soul of the old man in order to clothe it with the new, that which God has created completely new.* They called him *dumb* because he bore all the insults, threats and blows in silence.

As usual God was there. And He turned this bitter experience into an intense catalyst which drew John closer to Himself. He was now thirty five. He could examine himself and at the same time give new spirit to all that he had believed in until now.

Bereft of all human consolation, he had no choice but to look upwards. He realizes that God loves him and this is enough. *The purest suffering brings with it the purest understanding.* The nine months that he spent there were indeed nine months of gestation to a new life. *By emptiness and total aridity, God wishes to find out who the strong soldiers are who will fight and win his battle.* Even setbacks are a grace to the Christian. He received such great graces and heavenly light in prison that when he later described his experiences (even though he never goes into details) he affirms that for one of those graces he was willing to return to prison for years! How good God is! He never condemned the exaggerated severity of the prior: *he did this because he thought that that was the best thing for me!*

After six months in this sombre room, the friar who was in charge of him was changed. Father John of Santa Mary replaced him. He was a young friar who immediately began to alleviate somewhat the afflictions of the saint. He gave him a new shirt, more food, and even paper and ink on which to write. And so, by the light that entered his cell at noonday, he began to write and to live his poems. He wrote the first 31 stanzas of the Spiritual Canticle - a song of daring love. The images, the words and the symbols were drawn from his heart, for this was the only vista he had. This friar's creative genius gushed out through his contact with the harsh, demanding realities of life. Just when someone less full of God than he would have turned inwards into himself and become cynical about everything, John sang poems which are full of love and the highest poetic symbolism. God gives new eyes. These were nine months of pregnancy which brought to life a new Father John. Pain did not make him bitter but creative.

In the meantime outside, the bitter quarrel between Calced and Discalced was still going on. Father John was perhaps the least belligerent among them but it was he who most suffered its consequences. Almost all the friars who had been arrested were set free in a few days. He remained locked up for eight and a half months. While the others quarrel in the daylight, he suffers in silence and is beingstrenghtened within darkness. However, he had no intention of ending his life locked up behind four walls. In the middle of August 1578 he escapes. Quite an adventure ...which would make a good film!

He starts planning his escape. He studies the

geography of the place when descending to the refectory for the discipline, he loosens the screws of the door lock, he calculates with a thread tied to a string the height of the outer wall, he tore his blanket up to turn it into a long rope, and ... on the eve of the Assumption, at night, he manages to climb out of the balcony. However, once he had jumped out of the monastery he finds himself in the yard of the nuns who lived next door to the friars. He starts panicking because the walls were high and, should he be found there, the consequences would be very grim. He tries to climb repeatedly, and at last, hardly knowing how, he finds himself on top of one of the walls. He took a deep breath, jumped down outside, and went to sleep in the doorway of a house. He waited for sunrise and then went to knock at the door of the Carmelite nuns of El Carmen de San Josè. The mother superior at once let him in - there is an ill sister who needs to go to confession! It obviously did not occur to the Friars who went in search of him to seek him *within* the enclosure. When it was dark, a knight who was a friend of the convent came to fetch him. Now he is free. *Many are the troubles of the just man, but the Lord delivers him from them all,* says the psalmist.

I drank from the inner well springs of my Bridegroom

He did not lie low for long. As soon as he felt strong enough, he went to the General Chapter which the Discalced, in a desperate effort to save themselves from a premature death, had called at Almadovar del Campo. This was a meeting of brothers. At last they were together again. Perhaps now they could look to the future with more confidence. They decided to defend their case in Rome. As soon as the Papal Nuncio, Sega got to know of it, he was so enraged that he threatened to excommunicate all who had participated in the chapter!

Father John was nominated superior of El Calvario in Andalucia. Here the litigation was less furious and he could live far from his persecutors. A new land. New people. His life now took another turn. From now on he would find himself more and more involved in governing the religious family to which he himself had given birth.

He was not very happy here. Notwithstanding this, the time in Andalucia was a very creative moment for his spirit.

The region offered him an inspiring and tranquil environment in which to develop his charism as a writer. He is now 36 years old. He is mature. He had undergone many critical experiences in life which had led him to realize that man's life is too precious for it to be dumped away and wasted in trivialities. It is vital for man that he understands that he was not created to let his desires thrust him hither and thither but that he had been created to enjoy the vision of God. *Desires tire and harass the soul. They are like impatient children, always complaining, always wanting first one thing and then another from their mother. They are never satisfied.* On the contrary, God gratifies completely and delights the soul. Therefore, John's heart pours forth poetry - all poetry of love. He is mad with Love. He can only talk of love. One can touch the divine in his poetry.

He also wrote some "Billettes" - short sentences full of wisdom which he distributed to the nuns who went to him for confession. Later he wrote commentaries on his longer poems: **The Ascent of Mount Carmel, The Dark Night, The Spiritual Canticle, The Living Flame of Love.** He wrote hurriedly - in fifteen days, despite all his pastoral work, he writes the commentary on The Living Flame of Love. Sometimes he writes on his knees in an attitude of prayer. *Some of the ideas come from my mind, some were given to me by God.* Everything rests on his experience. In his room he has nothing but his breviary, a cross and the bible. That was enough. He wrote for his disciples. It never occurred to him to produce a study or to publish something. Despite this, he is perhaps the only writer in Christendom who is able to express the great wonders which await the man who lets himself go to God. God is an artist and whoever lives with him explodes with joy and passion.

His teaching contrasted sharply with the prevalent cultural milieu. Spain had just freed itself from the Moors. Granada was the capital city of the Inquisition. Religious fanaticism was rampant. It was a time when the fear of God, the fear of punishment, the fear of hell, dominated all other religious sentiment. Precisely for this reason, the insistence of Father John on love, on the possibility that man has to become familiar with God - he even says that man can *marry* God! - was dangerous and hazardous.

In Andalucia he continues his mission as superior. First at El Calvario (1578/79) where he wrote the verses of the poem 'The Dark Night', then in Baeza (1579-1582) as

49

the rector of the college he himself had founded. During this time his mother dies. Later he lives in Granada, first as prior, then as Vicar Provincial for Andalucia and finally again as prior. The Granada monastery was known as Los Martires. He calls hither his brother Francis who was now a widower, so that he could live and help with the work of the monastery; he is now fifty years old and *is the dearest person I have in this life,* John says. In the monastery Father John was admired for the tactful way in which he was able to create an environment of faith, love and confidence. For instance, he would not hesitate to lead the friars out to make their meditation in some wooded field. He knew how to keep a healthy balance. Saints always have a freedom which is mind boggling! His favourite pastime was to help the lay brother placing flowers before the statues of Our Lady and Saint Joseph.

Many of the friars admired him for his zeal keeping the spirit of the Order whole and his special care for the sick or those who were afflicted by spiritual problems. Money was no problem as far as the sick were concerned; he was willing to spend all that was necessary in order to relieve their suffering. He did not like flattery. Once a friar remarked to him: *You must be the son of a gardener, for you are so good at growing turnips. No, I am not even that .... I am the son of a poor weaver.* When Mary of the Cross asserted how much she respected him *because you carry my same surname - of the Cross,* he answered dryly : *I will respect you if you are truly a friend of the cross.* He would not hesitate to use drastic measures to bring down to earth a friar who was becoming too grandiose. *To fall in love with us, God does not look at the greatness of our soul but at the greatness of our humility.* Come to me all you.

He also had a strong sense of trust in providence ... something which created a lot of headaches to the procurators of his monasteries! On one occasion Father Juan Evangelista complained to him that the purse was empty. Father John was not perturbed: *So what? ! Today we shall fast!* The procurator was not overjoyed with this answer. A few moments later he returned to Father John's door to remind him that there were sick people in the monastery and that these needed something to eat. *Go and pray!* Father John replied, who knew that God loves the sick! Meal time arrived and the procurator still did not know what to do. *We are tempting God in this way. We must do something ... Will you give me permission to go outside to seek what is necessary?* Father John smiled: *Cetainly. Go and see how God will embarrass you!!* He had hardly stepped out of the door when he met Bravo, a messenger of the Udencia, who was coming to the monastery with 12 pieces of gold for the friars. This priest was so embarrassed that he did not even check whether they were *doblones* or *escudos!*

Apostolate was a significant part of his life, even more so when he himself began to taste the thrill of God. *O souls who were made for this, what are you doing? What are you spending time on? The Father wants to give us the same love He gives His Son ... This breath of the Spirit with which God transforms the soul into Himself is so fine and so sublime that no human tongue can explain it and no reason can understand it ...* He felt more at ease hearing confessions than preaching. Therefore we find him meeting all sorts of people - professors, university students, nobles, workers, women. At that time the superior was very much more involved in the activity of the Church. What he wrote to one nun was also the programme of his life: *One must take all his courage and risk on God. Let him remain faithful to the vows of his Order and then rest on God who will provide the necessities of life*.

However in a particular way, he worked closely with the cloistered nuns, especially since Mother Teresa had asked him explicitly to do so. He felt deeply attracted to the monastery which he had visited when he first arrived in Andalucia: Beas de Segura (Jaen). The superior, Mother Anna, who later became his intimate friend, was at first offended because Father John had called Mother Teresa *my Daughter*. When she wrote to Mother Teresa about this and mentioned the problem she had of not being able to find a confessor who was capable of guiding the nuns, Mother Teresa, with her usual sense of humour, answered her *You made me laugh when you complained without need since you have this,* my Father, *brother John of the Cross who is a divine and heavenly man.*

He would spend a great deal of time talking to the nuns about God, explaining the meaning of suffering and the tension-filled adventure of the soul searching for God. A favourite theme was his poetry, because the nuns often asked him the meaning of these verses. It was these discussions which led to his later writing commentaries on his poems. *He would speak of God with such fervor that it seemed he was seeing him!* - one of his companions remarked later. *Everyone had a good opinion of his spirituality and his joyful sincerity* - was the common opinion of the nuns.

The image of the mountain began to form in his mind. The mountain ... the place of the presence of God, the place where man, detached from everything, can discover himself and the One who loves him immensely. Mount Carmel ... the place where God lives. A mountain and a road - a road which leads to this God who is everything. A road which is not made of success or of pleasure but the basic road of nothingness. It is possible to pass along this road and meet Him. It is possible to live in heaven even in this life. The important thing is to know how to avoid the obstacles on the way. To embrace nothing in order to gain more easily everything. It was for the nuns of Beas that he drew the diagram of Mount Carmel with the famous verses: *If you wish to taste everything, aim to taste nothing; if you wish to know everything, aim to know nothing; if you wish to have everything, aim to have nothing ...!!* A forceful commentary on the words of the Master: *If you do not lose your life, you cannot find it.*

A few incidents. When the cook Sister Catherine of the Cross, a simple innocent woman, asked Father John why, when she passed beside the pond in the garden, the frogs always jumped into the water and hid, he answered that the pond was the place where they felt most secure - *You should do the same as well: escape creatures and throw yourself deep into the center which is God and hide yourself in Him.* A whole programme for life! *Why do you love so much the mass of the Holy Trinity?* these nuns once asked him. *Because the Trinity is the greatest saint in heaven!*

he replied. Once he layed down on the ground praying in the chapel. When he went to hear confessions, his face was shining with joy. *Why are you so happy?* he was asked. *Can I not be happy after seeing and adoring my Lord!? Oh what a good God we have!* On another occasion, when returning to his monastery, a woman with a child in her arms begged him for charity because she claimed he was the father of the boy! Father John, half seriously and half smiling, asked her who the mother was and how old the child was. His mother is a lady of the city, who has never left this city, and the boy is over a year old. *Then this is the son of a great miracle, for I have only been here a few months!* he replied, and he returned to the monastery to recount this adventure.

Let us taste the fresh juice of the pomegranates.

The last three years which he spent in Andalucia were outwardly years of much activity, but internally they were years of extreme tranquility. The closer he came to God, the more he realized that he knew nothing about Him. Indeed, he began to feel that his writing hid rather than exposed the mystery of God. God is too great. At the age of forty four he stopped writing completely. He began to feel the need to unite himself more closely with his Beloved. This was the aim of his life: to live in union with God and as he wrote himself *when the soul enters into union with God, it is not right that the soul should occupy itself with any other thought or work which might separate her even a little from that loving attention to God, even if these works should be for the spreading of his kingdom. A trifle of pure love is worth more and is much more precious in the eyes of God and of the soul than any other thing.*

However, God still wanted him to continue to work in his vineyard. In 1581 the Discalced finally achieved juridical separation from the Calced. This meant that they could now move forward. The sun had come out after the bitter night. Father Gracian, the provincial, much loved by Saint Teresa, called a chapter in Lisbon. In this chapter the new superiors were appointed. Father Doria, an Italian, was the new superior of the Order. Father John was chosen vicar provincial of Andalucia. This chapter was continued seven months later in Pastrana. A change of provincial meant a change in the programme of action. *I hope in God that even after my death, my bones shall shake in their grave and shout Regular Observance! Regular observance!* This Father Nicholas Doria was a priest of strong character, an honest man, but he wanted to impose the things of God by force. He was too much of a stoic to be a good superior. Too much perfection and too little compassion ... *The soul who lives in love is not aggravated and does not aggravate others,* Father John of the Cross used to say.

Now that he had become vicar provincial of all the monasteries of Andalucia, he had to travel a great deal because he had to visit all the monasteries regularly. Quite a lot of adventures also! Once he fell over a precipice and it seemed as if a hand helped him to climb up from where he had fallen. On another occasion he found himself involved in a knife fight between two men - *In the name of Jesus Christ I order you to stop* he called as he threw his hat between them. They were so surprised that they stopped and Father John was able to put some sense into their minds. Once, when a wall fell upon him, with a smile he claimed that the Virgin in a white cape covered him herself and so he survived without any injury.

At the end of 1588 he left Andalucia and went to Segovia. In the General Chapter of Madrid they in fact made him prior of this monastery and first Definitor of the Order. He was glad to go there because the place was secluded, desolate and quiet. Besides he was back in Castille ... which is where he had always wished to be. At last, it seems, his superiors took notice of his wishes. As soon as he arrived, he began to work on the building of a new monastery. *How you enjoy being among the lime and the stones!* some one remarked. *Don't be surprised, for here I have less of a chance of falling into sin than amongst men.* With ease he was able to unite manual work, apostolate, administrative work and an intense prayer life (he even spent whole nights praying out in the open air in summer). The closer one comes to God the more one becomes simple... like Him. Together with the rest of the definitory, he worked to publish the first edition of the works of Mother Teresa of Jesus.

God wished to move him further ahead. He himself had told Sister Anna of Saint Joseph *not to want anything but the stark cross, because this is something very beautiful*; and in the spring of 1590, when talking to his brother Francis, he recounted how once the crucified Jesus spoke to him saying *ask me whatever you want for I will give it to you for the service you have done me.* Father John had answered: *Lord, I pray that I should suffer much for you and to be despised and considered as nothing by others.*

Saint Paul used to say that the Christian is the trash of the floor and a spectacle of mirth for the world... When the time came, God gave him what he wished.

O night that has united the lover with his beloved.

John, a quiet retiring type, uninterested in diplomacy and the sterile cunning of men, found himself involved in the complicated machinations that Father Nicholas Doria, the vicar general of the new Order, was carrying out. He was too close to the central government of the Order. He had an important office and so often he had to intervene and speak clearly on controversial issues.

Basically he and Doria disagreed about the spirit of the Order. Doria believed in laws and their observance. John believed in the spirit of the charism and in freedom. In particular Father Doria had created the Consulta - a sort of centralized government which was meant to organize and lead all the nuns and dictate to them what they were to do. In her life Saint Teresa had always believed that men could never fully understand women, and had always wished that her monasteries should have some degree of autonomy. John knew this. He was also aware of the sensitivity and the spiritual needs of many of the nuns and the absurdity of having each problem discussed by the Consulta, kilometers away ... Thus, a confrontation was clearly in the air. Father Doria wanted to centralize, but Father John, alone among the Definitors, held out with a humble but strong resistance.

When Father Doria heard that the nuns had written

to Rome for a brief to protect their autonomy, he was so furious that he wanted to expel them from the Order. Father John disagreed, and said so clearly. Father Ambrose of Saint Mary, another definitor, teased him ironically: *Father John, when shall we see some wisdom in your bald head?* Father John was indeed bald. *When God wants to ripen it!!* answered John. He was not the touchy kind of person!

Another problem which arose and which increased the strain between Doria and John was the way the ex-provincial of the Order, Father Gracian, was being treated. He was being accused of many serious offences. Father Doria wanted to make these accusations public; Father John insisted on a more Christian line of action. Another thing which John could never stomach was the multiplication of laws which were being promulgated constantly by the Definitory. In four years, Father Doria issued over three hundred laws in his obsession to make everything precise and exact. Father John believed that the Teresian spirit would feel trapped in a cage of laws. *The spirit blows where it wills.*

The consequences were obvious. In the general chapter of Madrid (1591) Father John was not appointed for any office. This was exactly what the saint wished. But they had done this not to please him but because he had become too much of a nuisance for them. Twenty two years after the Reform, for the first time he was a simple friar ... and he thought he could now live in peace. But he was wrong. *If we do not use this life to become like God, it is worthless*, he wrote at that time to Sister Anna.

A real hurricane fell on him. Some friars who had long had a deep grudge against him, especially Father Diego Evangelista, started a campaign of calumny against him and began undertaking investigations in the convents where he had acted as spiritual director which caused quite an embarrassment to many of the nuns. He found himself defenceless. Many of his friends began to believe the rumours and left him. Meanwhile Father John, who had gone to the desert of La Penuela, received more bad news. His name was being ridiculed, rumours were being spread about him, there were even attempts to expel him from the Order. There was a point when it was thought best to get rid of him by sending him to Mexico. Few friends stood by him, and these had no authority.

His reaction is very interesting. Now his heart is full of God and so no one can upset him. In his heart, the night had passed and dawn was near. So we find him calm, full of respect for his enemies. He encourages his friends who were panicking: *My daughter, where there is no love, put love and you will draw forth love.* His letters in these months are an authentic exposition of divine psychology: *All is ordered by the provident hand of God. If we believe that it was He who multiplied the bread, why do we not think that we are protected by the same providence when people persecute us?* Obvious is it not? ! *Let our strength be in quiet and hope. Pray a great deal for me.*

He now became ill. He started to have a severe fever because of an inflammation in his leg. He was therefore forced to leave the desert in order to receive medical treatment. He was allowed to choose the monastery he wanted to go to: Ubeda, Beas or Granada. He chose Ubeda, where the prior, Father Francis Chrisostom, disliked him. He frequently reminded John of differences between them in the past, he was niggardly in giving John food, he prevented John having medicine.... John *of the Cross*. He had lived on it, now he wanted to die on it. This is not poetry!!

He was now at his end. He could no longer stand on his feet. He had to lie in bed, in great pain, because the tumor on his leg had enlarged and spread and began to produce much pus. Father Anthony of Jesus, his old companion in Duruelo, who is now provincial of Andalucia, hastens over to see him. He arrived on 27th November, the eve of the anniversary of the beginning of the reform and he started recounting to the friars of the monastery about those first days; but Father John silenced him and reminded him: *Had we not given our word never to speak about that time?* He loved silence. *And our Father, who sees what is done in secret will pay you Himself.*

He died happy. Many people began to come to see him. Often they brought him food. Others brought bandages for the wounds on his feet. The nuns sent him sweets made specially for him. Once it was even proposed to bring over some singers to make him forget his pain. All this was done in spite of the sullen looks of the prior who was constantly complaining about all these excessive favours and the cost of the medicines ... People began to ask him for his habit, his breviary, his scapular ... and he, with a smile told them not to ask for these things, as they were not his but belonged to the monastery. He burnt some letters of friends which he had in his possession. Whenever he opened his eyes he would look straight at the cross he kept in front of him.

The pain increased and he kept repeating *more patience, more pain, more love*. He asked pardon of those around him. On the eve of the Immaculate Conception,when the doctor warned him that he was dying, with enthusiasm he repeated in Latin the words of the psalmist *I rejoiced when they told me - we are going up to the house of the Lord*. Six days later, on December 13th, as the time of Matins approached, he turned to the infirmarian and said *Tonight I shall go to sing matins with the Virgin Our Lady in heaven.* The friars gathered round him. Some said that they saw a sphere of light on the ceiling. While he admonished his brother priests to be always obedient, he asked the superior to read him verses from the Cantares (The Song of Songs). *What beautiful pearls*, he remarked.

At midnight he heard the bells ring for Matins, grasped the crucifix, kissed it and ... opened his eyes in heaven. It was Saturday 14th December 1591. That day he found Everything and lost nothing. [10]

□

CHRIST CRUCIFIED
A Drawing by St. John of the Cross

His Message

John of the Cross had a vision.
A vision which he believed in
and which he lived.

That is why
his message is a vibrant message
which can enlighten us
in the problems and contradictions
which we experience every day.

In the following pages,
we are going to shed some light
on the vision this saint lived.

We are going to relate it to our life today.
It is today that we are living.
It is today that we need support.

This message was originally written
in the form of a dialogue between two people.

Join the dialogue.
Above all come close to the Lover
who is always so near to you ...

1 - TO LIVE OTHERWISE ... is possible

One of the best experts on Saint John of the Cross, the Englishman, Allison Peers, calls this saint *the mystic of mystics. Should these words frighten us?* he asks himself in the introduction to his excellent book **"Spirit of Flame"**. *No! There is no need for any apprehension!* he answers.

A mystic is a person who has fallen in love with God. We are not afraid of lovers - no indeed: 'all the world loves a lover'. They attract us by their ardour, their single mindedness, their yearning to be one with the object of their love. It was in just that way that Saint John of the Cross thought about God and strove after God, longing, too, that others would do the same.

/ Amazingly enough, when you start yearning for God you start yearning for man. You even start savoring nature which surrounds you. God encompasses all. The mystic embraces all.

In the small village of La Carolina (Jean) in front of the 'La Immaculada' Church there is an ecological statue of Saint John of the Cross. A rather unique statue. The Saint is sitting on some lumber and a little rabbit is trying to hide under his habit!

It recalls a pleasant, refined story. John of the Cross spent his last months of his life in Penuela, today La Carolina. A small monastery, a friendly community, a beautiful atmosphere of quiet and calm. He was happy and relaxed that he could work in the fields away from the bustle and complexity of Madrid.

One day Father Cristobal de Santa Maria was burning some dry branches in the fields around the monastery when suddenly the wind changed and all the crops started catching fire. The fire began to spread rapidly and started approaching dangerously close to the monastery. The friar, realizing the seriousness of the situation, threw himself into fighting the fire. He ended up *broken and dead* to use the expression of one of the Fathers who was there.

Meanwhile the bells had started ringing and all the Fathers were out trying to subdue the fire. Someone insisted that Father Prior should consume the consecrated hosts because they were afraid that the fire might destroy the entire building. Father John insisted that they should not panic! *Come on! We need the Blessed Eucharist because it is the Eucharist that is going to defend us!* Being the practical man he was, Father John soon organized the tasks - some were to stay kneeling down in front of the Blessed Sacrament praying, others were to collect the necessary belongings from the monastery, just in case the fire engulfed them, while the third group wrestled with the fire. He stationed himself where the flames were most furious. It was risky because the flames continued to spread with fury. But John stayed there without moving, talking with God.

In a little while, the fire, as if obeying an order, retreated and the flames began to burn out....

Once the danger was over, Father John arose and returned to the monastery. He entered into the cell of a friar who had been unable to leave his room because of his illness and jokingly told him: *It would have been a novel experience to die roasted by fire!!* Then he went to speak with the Prior, Father Diego de la Concepcion, who was fuming because of Father Cristobal's carelessness and with simplicity told him: *Father Prior, it is better if you soothe Father Cristobal and have some chicken soup made for him because he definitely needs it; look at him - he is exhausted and devastated."*

When things started to calm down, Brother Martin opened the doors of the church to let out the smoke which had filtered in. As soon as he opened these doors he saw a small rabbit who had found refuge in the Church. *As soon as I opened the door, the rabbit came out running towards the place where Brother John was with the other religious and hid beneath his habit. The fathers caught it and held it by the ears, but twice the rabbit managed to escape always running towards the saint, each time hiding beneath his habit ...*

It is an exquisite story. It happened in the last months of his life. It shows us how practical he was. It shows us also his refined gentleness with his brothers. Saints do not live detached four meters above the ground, in a nirvana of dreams and illusions. Their feet are well fixed to the ground. They know how to help out. They know how to be of service to others.

Furthermore, whoever lives close to God acquires a

harmony with nature itself - with trees, with flowers, with fire, with animals!

We are all attracted by nature. We all enjoy going for a walk among the fields or by the sea. Why does nature leave such a deep impression on us? True, it is beautiful, but there is a deeper, a more revealing reason.

Nature attracts us because it is innocent. Look into the eyes of a dog - there is a striking innocence. The innocence which man, who has made himself the god of his life, has lost. The innocence which the girl who has lost her virginity has lost. And without innocence there is no bliss! Life is as simple as that. Observe a photograph of yourself as a child, when your senses had not yet been sullied with pornography, with dirty jokes or the corrupt stupidity which television tries to make us swallow constantly. Look into your eyes when you were a child and the difference is remarkable!

The good news is that our Lord Jesus Christ can give us back this innocence. Jesus Christ came so that he could win back for us that proximity with God which we, in our madness, lost. The dead burden of sin may cling to us like glue. But Jesus Christ has the power to free us from this stigma and make us new again. Completely fresh. He did not come to patch the disorder or to repair the havoc but to create a new man. A new nature. He wants to generate us afresh.

It is possible to live differently. It is possible to be energized again. It is possible to be young ... even though the years may pass.

This is why Saint John of the Cross could sing songs of love in such a passionate and fervent way. Our hardened ears may feel confused. Our sins may have made us old. But a lover is always young. John addresses God and dares to tell him this:

"Lord God my beloved! Give me without delay that which I ask you! Do not remember my sins but exercise your goodness and mercy on them. Do not await my good works: do these for me yourself.

Allow the sufferings which you wish me to accept to come upon me. For how can a man begotten and nurtured in lowliness rise up to you, Lord, if You do not raise him with the hand which made him?

Do not take away from me, my God, what you once gave me in your only son, Jesus Christ, in Whom you gave me all I desire. Hence I rejoice because I know that if I wait for you, you will not delay.

Yes mine are the heavens and mine is the earth. Mine are the nations, the just are mine, and mine the sinners.

The angels are mine, and the mother of God, and all things are mine; and God himself is mine and for me because Christ is mine and all for me.

What do I ask then and what do I seek once this is all mine and all for me?

O my God, teach me not to engage myself in something less or pay heed to the crumbs which fall from my Father's table. But grant that I shall go forth and exult in my glory! So I shall ever more hide myself in You and exult in you!" [11]

The Saint called this prayer *"The prayer of a soul in love with God"*. He who realizes how Jesus Christ is able to give him back purity of heart and zeal for life, inevitably enters into a tumultuous love story with him.

But if we want to delve deeper, we shall discover that there is yet another reason why we are so attracted to nature. In nature we see obedience. The sun does not contend with God, but daily it shares its heat and its warmth. Trees and flowers always give us their fruit and their beauty. Stones stay where they are put. Animals know how to show their gratitude to those who love them without demanding a lot.

He who does not obey is not alert because without obedience one cannot love. If you love your wife, you have to obey her and if you love your parents you obey them. Because love is relationship with the other; it is I who give myself to the other. And this is impossible without obedience.

In love it is not I who count but the other. So much so that one can taste ecstasy only when one crucifies oneself for others. God created nature in his image. He created us in His image. Each cell in our body was created in his image. And the image of the Son of God is a body stretched out on a cross. A body resting on the bed of a cross out of love for mankind. This crucified body was raised from the dead. To live this love is heaven. This is the only reality.

This is the banner which we Christians must raise before our generation. It is not true that you are happy when you sin. It is not true that you are happy when you are caged in by your egotism. No this is not true!

69

True happiness means receiving this spirit of Jesus Christ, this crucified and victorious love. And this can only come from heaven.

We have no reason to be afraid of our Lord. Jesus Christ is very good. Saint John of the Cross is a valid witness of this basic truth. God never ran him down. He always encouraged him. When others turned their back on him, and reproached him and were gripy about him, Jesus Christ always told him: *Courage! I love you. I care for you!*

This love of Jesus Christ won John over. It can win *you* over. He is the most handsome, He is the best, He is the bridegroom. He who finds Christ finds life. He who finds Christ is never alone, even if he is on a sick bed, even if his children have abandoned him in an old people's home, even if he has remained single all his life.

But, he who has not found Christ - even if he has a beautiful wife and three children and people idolize him and has reached the top and is rolling in money .... if he has not found Christ, I am very sorry for him, he is alone. Alone. He is condemned to rummage everywhere and always for a little bit of pleasure, a little bit of gratification. He craves to be loved. He tries to wallow in pleasure because only thus can he feel loved. And so he tries drugs, gets involved in power struggles, seeks sex, passes hours before the television, eats and eats. He cries a lot. Always lonely and miserable.

Outside God, everything is tasteless, Saint John of the Cross used to say. How right he was! Only He can come over to meet you in your situation and tell you: *Rise, rise my dove and come, come.* Rise from your sin, rise from your death and let us go to Jerusalem to eat the fruits of innocence and of obedience.

And so we become young .... even if our hair is white and we have wrinkles on our faces. For love keeps us always fresh and youthful.

In the Spiritual Canticle the Saint writes thus about this fully fledged love.

> *With flowers and emeralds*
> *chosen on a cool morning,*
> *we shall weave garlands*
> *flowering in your love,*
> *and bound with one hair of mine.*

And he comments : *The flowers are the soul's virtues, and the emeralds are the gifts she has received from God. These flowers and emeralds are chosen on cool mornings. This means they are acquired at the time of youth, which is life's cool morning. She points out that they are chosen, because she obtained them during her youth when the vices put up more strenuous opposition and nature is more inclined and ready to lose them; also by beginning to gather the virtues, at this early season, she acquires more perfect and choice ones.*

How lucky we are that God has set his eyes upon us!

2 - A GAME OF LOVE

We cannot live without a vision. Man, any man or woman, has a project which determines his or her life. Some live for one thing, others for another.

Saint John of the Cross had an enormous vision - a vision that can be yours! He believed that man was created for love. Without love, nothing makes sense, nothing has flavour.

He believed that God made man for only one purpose: God wishes to live united with men. He even dares to use a strong expression which said by him does not have any innuendo of a poetic symbol but of a convincing vital reality. He dares to say that God wants to *marry* man. He wants to marry you and me!

You marry the person you love most. You marry the person whom you consider as the most beautiful and precious in your eyes. You marry the person without whom you feel life would be impossible to live. God feels all this when he ponders about man!

In this union, the soul submerges itself in a deeper way in God - and He gives himself even more fully to her. Passionate love on the part of God. Passionate love on the part of man. A passion which leads to total union between God and man.

The Saint prefers the word *union* to the word *perfection,* because *union* is more dynamic, more alive.[12]

Perfection implies the law, something cold and dead; it implies stress and effort . *Union* on the other hand means togetherness, **love**. It means necessarily two persons, a relationship which grows and develops. It means self giving by God and self giving by man. It means a tension of love.

"Every wish and aim of the soul - and of God - in all its works, are the end and completion of this state, therefore the soul does not tire until it comes to this state ... Now it is resting in the arms of its beloved, by whom she feels embraced continually in the spirit. This embrace is real and through it the soul lives the life of God."

Here we are not talking of some symbolic image or fairy tale abstraction. This is not a simulation but a reality. You can be the protagonist of this adventure of love. Christian life is not obey - live a respectable life - be a good boy - and go to heaven if you have followed the rules... but it is a game of love. I can live this experience in my flesh.

Saint John of the Cross is a practical man. And he is speaking from his own living experience. It is possible to enter into such a deep intimacy with Jesus Christ that he becomes your bridegroom, the beloved of your heart, and you become his 'unique' loved one. *First of all, we must say that if a soul seeks God, even more so does the beloved seek her.*

Fray Jeronimo de la Cruz, the Saint's companion, stated in the apostolic process for his beatification which was held in Jaen, that *on journeys he would normally read something ... The servant of God had the custom to keep repeating in a quiet recollected voice, the seventeenth chapter of the Gospel of Saint John. This he did with great devotion, which he would also transmit to his companions.* He knew this chapter by heart.

The seventeenth chapter is the prayer of Jesus for his apostles. It is a prayer of intimacy between the Son and the Father where Jesus looks on his great friends and asks the Father to give them the gift that *they recognize you, the one true God and Jesus Christ whom you have sent* and most of all he insists that the Father *protects them so that they be one as we are one.* A very momentous prayer indeed: *As you are in me, Father, and I in you, so may they be also one IN US, so that the world may believe that you have sent me!* One just feels stunned simply thinking of this vision which the Father has of us!

For Saint John of the Cross, union with God means union with **Jesus Christ**. His God is not an ethereal being up in the skies. He is a person who entered into the history of mankind. He is a person who, driven by his love for us *did not consider equality with God a thing to be grasped, but he emptied himself taking the form of a servant.* [13]

This is the adoption of the children of God who can continually say to God what his own Son said to the divine Father: 'All that is mine is yours, and all that is yours is mine' (John 17,10). Jesus says this in an essential way because he is the natural son, we say this in a participative way because we are adopted sons. So he said these words not just for himself, the head, but also for the whole mystical body which is the Church. The church will have the chance to participate in the very beauty of the bridegroom on the day of her victory, when she sees God face to face. Therefore the soul prays that they should go and see themselves, she and the bridegroom, in his beauty alone. [14]

Union also means **presence**. When you love someone you want to be with him all the time.

Being the smart teacher that he is, the Saint explains this thought very well: *Appear to me at once! In order to understand those words, we must know that God can be present in the soul in three ways.*

We know that God, first of all, is in us to give us life. If God were to leave us we would vanish, we would cease to exist! God is also within us through grace. When we are in the grace of God, God lives in our soul content and pleased with us. Those who fall into serious sin lose this presence.

However there is another presence which is more important - this occurs by a spiritual empathy. Here there is intimacy, union, love, passion. Here God is in us to console us, to soothe us and to gladden us. *The third presence occurs by a spiritual affinity, because God gives to many devout souls manifestations of a spiritual presence by which he consoles them, has mercy on them and makes them happy.*

To take one small example, not every married couple is equally close. There are some who really love and who therefore feel united with the partner, they enjoy being together, they enjoy sharing their problems with each other and enjoy staying at home or going out together. Others, even though married and living under the same roof, do not relish the idea of being together. Maybe they argue too much, maybe their love has gone cold, maybe there is another woman or man involved ... one thing is certain; although they live physically close together, the fact is that they are far apart. In other words, there are different kinds of presences!

God wishes to be present to us in the same way as a man who loves his wife wishes to be present to her. To use John's own words: *O sweetest love of God so little known! Whoever has found its source has found rest!*

All is a gift. All is grace.

It is indeed a great joy to the soul when it understands that God never leaves the soul, not even when it is in serious sin; much less obviously when it is in God's grace.

In this way man discovers his roots. While he was commenting on the eighth stanza of the Canticle: *How do you endure O life, not living where you live,* John asserts, *besides this life of love through which the soul that loves God lives in Him, her life is radically and naturally centered in God.*

Yes, union means intimacy. Union means being united with Jesus Christ. Union means presence. Union also means **communication.** For the presence of God is an active presence. God enjoys playing this game of love with man.

God seeks out man, he catches him, heals him and transforms him into Himself. He makes man look like Him. Yes, it is possible to resemble God himself! *When there is union in love, His image is so imprinted in the soul that we can indeed say that the beloved lives in the soul and she lives in her beloved. Love causes such a resemblance to come about in the lovers that we can say that one is transformed into the other and that they become one. The reason for this is because in this union and this transformation, one gives himself to the other and each one wants to convert himself into the other. So each one lives for the other, and one is the other and the two become one in a transformation of love.*

How realistic the saint is!

In this interior union, God gives himself to the soul with such a sincere love that there is no love of a mother yearning for her child, or brotherly love, or friendship which can be compared to this. This is the extent of the truth and the tenderness with which the immense Father cares for and nurtures this soul full of love. O how wonderful, deserving of fear and admiration, that He ministers indeed to the soul to nourish it, as if He is her servant and she His master! And He is so willing to caress her as if He were her slave and she His God! So profound is the humility and sweetness of God.

These words bring real solace to our souls. More and more when we realize that even you and I can live this same vision.[15]

3 - THE ONLY ONE WHO REALLY LOVES US

Joseph had been trying to move this block of stone for some time. His face was bright red, all covered with sweat. But the stone did not budge one millimeter. It was too heavy. His father passed by and was bemused at his little boy trying to push such a huge stone. He smiled and said: *Joseph, are you using all your strength? Yes father,* answered the other. *Don't you see how I am all covered with perspiration...?* But the father shook his head and said: *No, my son, you are not using all your strength.* The lad was perplexed because he was certainly tired out. *No, my son,* repeated his father. *You are not using all your strength because you have not yet asked me to help you.*

Indeed, the strength of the father becomes the strength of the son as soon as the son asks the father to help him. And any father enjoys helping his children.

Often, far too often, the same thing happens to us in our relationship with God. Faced with our life with all its problems we try to cope by ourselves. We try to go on in our own strength. We reason things out with our mind alone. Therefore we get tired and at the end of the day we find ourselves shattered, ever more alone, ever more depressed and discouraged. With a lot of question marks flaring through our mind.

If only we learnt to ask our Father in heaven to help us more often, then life would become easier, and indeed, more beautiful, because we would not be alone, with our rundown strength, trying to move the rocks of our problems but there would be God himself who would shift the boulders of our problems for us.

If only we learn to involve God more in our lives!

This was one of the profound intuitions of Saint John of the Cross. He believed that God cares about man. Not only does he care, but he wants to intervene in our life to help us. Our God has big heart!

Listen to two witnesses among many. *It seems to me that of all the mysteries, the one he loved most were the Holy Trinity and that of the Incarnation of the Son of God. I often watched him say the mass of the Holy Trinity, and once I asked him 'Why do you say the mass of the Holy Trinity so often?' And he answered me, not without a smile on his lips 'Because I think that this is the greatest saint in heaven!'*

During the process for his beatification, while they were collecting testimonies about him, one friar said *He used to say that the effect of the habitual presence of the Lord our God is that his soul was taken into the depths of the Holy Trinity; and in the company of this mystery of the three divine persons, his soul would indeed acquire great benefits.*

What does he mean by all this? Something very simple. He believed, since he had experienced it in his life, that God is never far away from man. God does not want to, indeed he cannot, stay distant from man, for the simple reason that God loves man, and he loves him enormously.

One of the very strong images which Saint John of the Cross uses to try to describe the caring power of God is *the stag!* He says that God is a stag! Because as he comments in his typical fresh style: *When the stag hears the cry of its mate and sees that she is wounded, he hurries to her and comforts her and encourages her. This is what the Bridegroom does.*

As soon as God hears the anguished cry of anyone, he moves. He approaches us. And he is ever ready to dirty his hands, even with blood if necessary, in order to heal me. He is the Only One who always thinks positively about me. My wound becomes his wound.

Being the ardent poet he is, John of the Cross continues using images taken from nature which surrounds us in order to try to express something about the person he loved so much in the depths of his heart. In one of his poems, **The Living Flame of Love,** he compares God with *a flame of fire.* A flame which enfolds us.

This is the truth: we are swimming in love! The air that we are breathing now is love and if we lack air, we die. The birds, the clouds, the world, everything is filled with the holiness of God. God is indeed giving himself totally and continuously to us!

I myself am a masterpiece of God. He not only created me because he loves me but he gave me many, many things. He showed me how much he loved when he gave me eyes, mouth, hands, feet. It is not me who is keeping my heart beating. It is not me who is making my brain work. It is not me who is making my lungs pump constantly. My heart, veins, blood, bones, nervous system ... everything is amazing, everything was given to me freely.

The problem is that we are living in a society which says that God is dead and therefore we are gods. Therefore we can decide ourselves on our life, we can kill, we can do what we like.

We have pushed God aside and therefore nothing has meaning. Everything has become a hassle. The heat bothers us, the wind troubles us. Marriage annoys us. Noises bugs us. Silence irks us. We gripe too much. We have become a people who is never satisfied.

The fault is not entirely ours. Our society is a pitiless society. It forces us to build our lives on money, production, work. And so man has become a machine ˇ always on the go, always breathless. We do not have time even to appreciate life around us.

Saint John of the Cross, precisely because he learnt to put God into the centre, managed to open new horizons even for us: *in this state of perfect life, the soul is, both outwardly and inwardly, always celebrating and from its mouth there pours forth a voice of divine joy ˇ like a song which is always new, full of joy and love.*

Indeed one may say that here the soul is clothed in

God and swims in divinity, not only exteriorly but in the very depths of its spirit. In a society which, as it advances further in what is termed 'progress', is feeling less and less the need of God in its life, the witness of John of the Cross is precious because he constantly reminds us that *outside God everything is anguish* and *the soul cannot be content with anything less than God.*

A certain type of church has not helped much to clarify this situation. Far too often from our churches there has issued a smell of the mortuary, as if we are witnesses of a dead man rather than of one who is risen from the dead! The mourning and resignation of many Christians suffocates the search of those who wish to discover life and joy!

The passionate nature of John of the Cross is a strong cry calling us to rise out of our slumber. It tears through the cynical pessimism which often paralyses us. His witness is one of joy˘ *The soul not only rests in a bed of roses which is nothing else but the Bridegroom himself, but also in the rose itself which is the Son of God, in which there is a divine perfume and grace and beauty ...*

What can I do?

I could continue struggling along in my usual path, hoping that this comedy of life will end soon. Or I could choose the same path which Saint John of the Cross took and see what I can do to make God more important in my life.

We strive so much for money. We work so hard for health. We study so much and talk to so many people to achieve the aims we have in mind. If we only spent half of this energy and of half of this time to learn to know better and love more the God who loves us so much, then laughter will appear more frequently on our faces.

For as our Saint says, *He who loves does not tire nor does he tire others.* It is beautiful to live with the living God. This is the secret of everything. God was the oxygen of his life. He could become the oxygen of your life.

4 - A lover of God

Que bien Dios tenemos! - this expression was often on the lips of Saint John of the Cross. *How good, how sweet is our God!*

For Saint John of the Cross, God was not an academic subject. An object of mental curiosity. Before being a theologian, he was a mystic - a man who has experienced God.

For him God was someone. A person. Someone who knows how to love. And because He knows how to love, He knows how to give himself. *God is like a spring from which each one may drink his fill.* The secret of everything is this love of God which from eternity wished, predestined and created man so that man can take part in the life of God himself. The secret of everything is this love of man which before this mystery, is silent and reaches out towards Him.

Happy the soul who loves, because she has God for a prisoner, ready to give her all that she wants! God has this quality: those who take him at his word and in love force him to do whatever they wish; but if they act towards him in a different way, they can neither talk to him nor do they have any power over him ...

This statement of the saint is a precious gem. God has *this quality* - he says - this way of action, this psychology ... It is important to know this because our life only makes sense if we are willing to enter His world. *They can neither speak to him nor do they have any power over him,* and he adds *even if they make exaggerated efforts.* This is a very radical statement. It is not rites and penances which have an impact on God's heart. Only love and deference reach Him. In the San Juanist vision, the heart is everything.

When he attempts to explain who God is for him, Saint John of the Cross finds himself before a mystery. *Un no sè que* he puts it delicately in Spanish. A mystery of extraordinary beauty. God is very close to us to the extent that *He is in you or better, you cannot be without Him.*

Eternal Father is what the Saint calls him to illustrate at the same time the idea of familiarity and intimacy and the idea of Someone else who is greater. *The immense Father,* a deep mine in which, no matter how deep you delve, you can never reach the bottom.

In the **Living Flame** he states that we are drawn to God as everything is drawn to its centre. For God is the centre of man.

Without realizing it, every man is seeking God. He feels drawn to everything that is beautiful, to all that is good, to all that is beauty. This is basically a search for God even in the night of pain, even in the darkness of a life which makes no sense and which sometimes crushes us with its weight.

But if it is true that man, whether he knows it or not, is searching for God, since after all God is the only one who can make sense of life, it is also true that God is madly in love with man. God enjoys giving, or better still He enjoys auto-giving, giving Himself.

He never tires of giving, Saint Teresa of Jesus liked to say. God loves more and loves better. So He searches for us more. Therefore, it is always He who makes the first, second and third step towards us.

There is a pre-history of love which is overwhelming. We often think of the beginning of our life as the day of our birth - or at most, nine months before. But this is only a fragment of our story. A very small particle. Because we were in the mind and heart of God from all eternity. Indeed, from eternity He wished us, loved us, and chose us. *The soul has thousands of benefits from before she is born.*

Nothing happens because it was destined to, or by

chance, or because I was born under an ill star or with a
favourable horoscope ... It is bewildering what stupidities
man can believe in, once he loses contact with God!

John the poet tries to express this story of love in the
Romances. These are nine theological poems of impressive
intensity about the Trinity and the Incarnation. For him
the Trinity is not a dry abstract idea which feeds the mind
but three living persons who warm our hearts with love.

> *My son, I wish to give you*
> *a bride who will love you.*
> *Because of you she will deserve*
> *to share our company*
> *and eat bread at our table,*
> *the same bread I eat.*

God created man to offer to His Son as his bride.
Thus man will be able to eat at table with the family of the
Trinity. Jesus himself came into being to be my bridegroom!
I was created so that I could eatat   the table of God!!!

In front of this mystery, the mystic sings.

> *In the beginning the Word*
> *was; He lived in God....*

For him God is not so much the person who created the
cosmos as He who loves.

> *Three persons, and one beloved*
> *among all three*
> *one love in them all*
> *makes of them one lover.*

They are one family who love each other all the time and therefore give themselves all the time to each other.

And the more love is one
the more it is love.

Precisely because God is love, he pours himself out to unite himself to us. God expands himself to embrace man in Himself!

The saint puts these words on the lips of the Father:
My son, I will give Myself
to him who loves You,
and I will love him
with the same love I have for You.

And in the Canticle he comments beautifully and delicately: *When God loves the soul, he is in some way placing it within Him, and encompassing it in him, and so He loves the soul in him and for Him with His own love with which He loves Himself.*

He is God-Trinity really close to man. A family who is passionately in love with us to the point of folly ...

It is cardinal to keep this in mind if we wish to understand the message of this Saint. Once man discovers love, he discovers a precious jewel; and once he discovers a precious jewel, he does not find it difficult to sell all he has to gain this jewel.

If we do not understand this, all becomes moralism

and senseless effort. I am willing to leave all behind me only because I have found a treasure: at last I have found someone who loves me just as I am, without expecting anything from me, someone who is not only ready to give his life for me, but who has already given his life for me when I did not even know him and did not even care for him. Whoever discovers this love is saved.

O Lord my God, who shall seek You with pure simple love, and will not find You as he has desired and wanted you, since You show Yourself first and You go out to meet those who wish for You?

The Christian life is always an answer to the initiative of God.

To clarify what the content of this loving attention of the soul is, he once wrote a note to a nun saying: *It is very wrong to keep your eyes on the good things of God more than on God himself.*

God remains always *el principal agente* - He who starts, *el principal amante* - he who loves first and above all.

How can we not fall in love with Him?! Especially when we realize that what moves God in our favour is not something good which we have in ourselves, but on the contrary it is the love of God which creates what is good in man. While people are attracted to us because they see some thing beautiful in us - and therefore human love is always tainted with egoism - God was attracted to us when we were bad and wicked ...

Stanza 33 of the Canticle is a gem. Even if *You found me dark* because of sin, *now truly you can look at me since you have looked and left in me grace and beauty.* And as the fine theologian he is, he comments *the soul is conscious that in herself there is no reason, nor possibility of a reason, why God should look at her and exalt her, but that this reason is only in God, in his mere will and beautiful grace.*

Just before he had just commented, *When You looked at me You made me pleasing to Your eyes and worthy of Your sight ...*

All is a free gift. This is God. He gives Himself to us freely without expecting anything in return. He wants no payment for His love.

And when He gives Himself, He fills man with gifts. *The look of God performs four good actions in the soul. It cleans it, it beautifies it, it enriches it and it enlightens it. Like the sun,* adds Saint John of the Cross the artist!

When God loves more, He gives more favours" And he repeats again a little later *Because with Your glance You place in my soul worth and beauty which cause You to esteem my soul and be drawn to it.*

When God in His mercy bends down to the soul *He carves it and marks it with His love and His grace with which He beautifies and raises it to make it a companion in His divinity.*

And more...

God loves as only God can love. In the **Flame** John produces a very valid principle: *When one loves ... he loves according to his condition.* The poor as a poor man , the rich as a rich man, man as a man, woman as a woman. Therefore God loves as only God can love! Let us listen to his words ....

Because your Bridegroom is within you, He gives you graces as befits Himself. Since He can do everything, He loves you and cares for you as one who can do everything; since He is wise. He cares for you and loves you with great wisdom; since He is good, you realize that He loves you with great goodness; since He is holy, He loves you and fills you with graces of holiness; since He is just he loves you with justice; since He is merciful, kind and compassionate, you experience His mercy, his kindness, and His compassion; since He is strong, gentle and delicate, you realize that He loves you with strength, gentleness and much delicacy.

And he continues ...

Since He is transparent and pure, you understand that He is loving you with great purity and cleanliness; since He is true, you realize that He loves you indeed; since He is generous, you realize that He loves you with great generosity and gives Himself to you without seeking His own interest, only thinking of your good; finally because He is the pinnacle of humility, He loves you with great humility and esteems you very greatly and wishes to make you like Himself. In this way He looks on you with a smiling face full of joy and tells you to your joy: "I am yours and for you. I am happy that I am who I am in order to give myself the better to you and to be truly yours." [16]

It is God who speaks thus. God Himself, the Lover, who seems to be lost in an ecstasy of love for man. God loves as only God can love! A blazing flame.

Such words are mind and heart boggling! God lost in an ecstasy of love. Here we are touching the very heart of the Gospel. We are touching the very heart of God. God is happy that He is God because this means that He can give more. Like a millionaire who is glad that he has so much money because in this way He can buy more things for those whom He loves.

The poet and the theologian in Saint John of the Cross fuse into each other to produce this mysticism. They become an ecstasy of love.

He is aware that many will not understand him simply because they have never truly experienced the God of Jesus Christ. Therefore, when he comes to comment on **The Living Flame**, which is a poem which is aglow with this union between God and man at its very extreme limits, he says at once: *We must not be surprised that God should give such high and such beautiful graces to souls, for once we consider that these favours are given in love and goodness by God as God, this does not appears so strange.*

Let us repeat. God loves as only God can love! As a billionaire and a herculean benefactor ...

We are facing a mystery. But not a mystery to our minds but to our hearts. This is why Saint John of the Cross does not feel disheartened, but on the contrary he throws himself even deeper into this abyss, convinced that he who has found God has found everything and that he who has found everything is in need of nothing more. *Who can say what is the greatness to which God exalts the soul whose company he enjoys? We cannot even dream it.*

He tries, but knows that he will be unable to express it. He tries to paint this vision of his in many beautiful colours with the hope that we too will be encouraged to open our hearts to this adventure . Indeed God is a feast!

That which God communicates to the soul in this intimate union cannot be described and we cannot say anything about it, as we cannot describe God himself. For God Himself communicates Himself to the soul and brings about a wonderful glorious transformation of the soul in Him. Thus the two become one as we could say of the rays of sun upon a glass pane, a spark and a fire, or of the light of the stars which is absorbed by that of the sun. However, this thing cannot take place ... in a total way.

All this comes about through the work of the Holy Spirit. *This change is not a true change unless the soul is changed by the three persons of the Holy Trinity in a clear and evident way.*

Much patience, much determination, a great vision, much optimism ... on the part of God. *And so the soul becomes like God and God like the soul!*

If only you and I had in us even a tiny glimmer of the enthusiasm that God feels for us! Life would be more restful and enjoyable...

5 - THE MOST HANDSOME!

Christmas meant a great deal to Saint John of the Cross, because he was overwhelmed when he contemplated how this God bends down so much towards man as to become man Himself. *The more he lowered himself for me, the dearer he is to me,* as saint Bernard says in one of his sermons. In Jesus Christ our Saint sees how practical and realistic God's love for man is.

God who had everything, gives up everything in order to give us the chance to be filled with everything. God who becomes a baby, who cries, who needs other men, who has to grow up, who needs to learn, who discovers nature, who runs, is obedient, eats, jokes, laughs, forms relationships, suffers, speaks out clearly, cares, dies ..... This is something which is indeed impressive.

And the amazing thing is that Jesus of Nazareth did all this not for Himself but for us. He gained nothing; indeed He lost everything. He loved us more than He loved Himself. Jesus is indeed the living icon of charity.

Hence the cross becomes the last manifestation and the greatest statement of Jesus Christ. His greatest act of love. Just when He was at His weakest, He performed the greatest deed He could ever do. When He was just a nonentity - people were laughing at Him, all had deserted Him, no consolation coming from anywhere, even His Father had abandoned Him in a fearful aridity - He carried out His most wonderful deed. In our favour.

This is why Saint John believed that it is impossible for us to walk the road that leads to the Father unless we constantly keep our eyes on Jesus Christ.

Look carefully at Christ and in him you will find that more has already been done and said than you might imagine. If you are expecting a word of consolation from me, look at my Son, He always obeys Me and for my love He accepted what was being said about him and He was tried, and so you will listen to how many questions He will answer for you. If you wish Me to show you things and happenings which are hidden, keep your eyes on My son, and there you will find the most profound mysteries, the wisdom and wonder of God ... Furthermore, if you seek some vision or divine revelation or any other thing, look at Christ the Son, and there you will find more than you might expect, for as Saint Paul states: 'In Christ the fullness of the divinity was pleased to dwell'.

Each word and action of the life of Christ contains within them great riches of salvation. These words alone are able to enlighten our lives. The saint learns to walk with Jesus because in Him he sees a sure guide who gently trains him in the mysterious paths which lead to the Father.

Jesus trains John by revealing to him the plans of

love that His Father has for mankind, the way He works in human history, all the possibilities which are open to the man who is willing to plunge himself into this adventure.

To express this thrilling venture, John uses two images : the image of the shepherd and that of the bridegroom. Saint John of the Cross is so adept at using biblical imagery!

In the Canticle he unites both images together: *The bridegroom had such a great wish to set the bride free from sensuality and the devil, that, now that he has freed her, he acts like the good shepherd who is full of joy when he carries the lamb on his shoulders ...;* in this way, this shepherd and bridegroom of our soul *amazes us with the way He rejoices and the delight He feels when he sees the soul won over, perfected and placed upon His shoulders.*

A shepherd who recognizes his sheep, who loves, cuddles, nurtures, guides and plays with his sheep ... A bridegroom who chooses his bride, fills her with riches, coaches her, forgives her and makes her as handsome and as mighty as himself!

Indeed Christ is everything. *Christ is like a mine with many shafts, full of treasures, into which, although one might enter deeply, one can never find the bottom or the end, indeed one keeps finding new veins and new riches here and there at every entrance.*

Christ is so much everything, that in order to restrain those who are constantly looking for more sensational objects, visions, devotions, extraordinary stuff... John states bluntly *since in Christ, the Father has shown us all the truths of faith, He will never have any more truths to show us."*

Indeed, they would be greatly offending my beloved Son if they were to expect special visions. After the revelation of His Son, the Father *has become dumb, so to speak, because He had nothing more to say.*

Now for man, a long journey of transformation begins. It is a journey *at the pace of man,* where the Christian slowly begins to participate in the very life of God. It is a journey which only a few people ever end. Many never even begin it.

One day, when out on a walk, Brother John asked Brother Martin, *Brother Martin, let's say that some people were to attack us now and treat us badly and beat us with sticks, what would you do?! Well,* the brother answered with great simplicity, *by the grace of the merciful God, I would accept the blows with patience. What!* cried out Father John, *are you so cold!? Don't you have a desire to suffer martyrdom for our Lord Jesus Christ? If this were to happen to us, we ought to encourage them to strike us even harder in order to make us martyrs for Jesus, our Redeemer...*

This is a story which can only be understood by those who know what Jesus Christ had done for them. Those who consider Jesus Christ as a devotional, pious, being - someone who is there so that when they need something, he is readily accessible, obviously cannot understand anything.

But those who know from what the Lord has saved them, can well understand this story. Sin activated death within us. It delivered us into the grave, ornate on the outside but stinking within. Sin shackled our feet and so we could not walk in the path of salvation, it chained our hands and so we could not love others, it blindfolded our eyes and so we could not perceive anywhere the love of God.

But Jesus Christ came ... and cried: *Lazarus come forth.* And he brought us out of our vices, out of our neurosis, out of our egoism. And he walked with us with much tenderness, compassion and emotion.

In a very forcible way, one of the leading Fathers of the Church expressed himself so: *You came down to earth Lord, to set Adam free, and when you did not find him, you went down to hades to seek him there. The Lord came down to seek you but he did not find you, so he went down, he went down further into the depths of your life ... With his light he enlightens the darkness within you, he draws you out of the grave of suffering, he destroys the latches of your passions, of your problems, of all those chains that prevent you from being free .. And he lifts you up so that you can start LIVING!*

How delightful it is to walk with Him! He makes sure you lack nothing! He constantly reassures you of His love. He is patient with your faults. Infinitely rich in mercy.

It is not surprising that the two pieces of advice which John of the Cross gives to those who seriously want to enter into this intimacy with Jesus Christ are both very powerful.

Those who search for God must always have a deep desire to constantly walk in the steps of Jesus Christ in all things. This is the first counsel. Indeed, the disciple is he who slowly, with a lot of patience but with great determination, enters into empathy with Jesus Christ in such a way that he begins to reason, think, love, dream and speak like Jesus Christ. Without any discordant note. Obviously, this is not a day's work, but a project that can only be realized gradually.

The second counsel which he proposes is also very powerful: *To model your life on the life of Christ, you must learn to detach your self from all that gives you pleasure, because the important thing is not to have kicks but to always do the will of God.* This is the true bread which feeds and satisfies man.

In other words, you cannot possibly pass all your life musing how to satisfy your whims and vagaries. You will never resemble your Master in this way! You will never be free as he was free. You will always remain a slave to your hankerings which will drive you hither and thither, constantly doing not what your mind and heart tells you, but what your instincts demand.

The Saint believes that the more one knows Christ the more one learns to love him, and the more one loves him, the more the desire would grow to be like him and to please him in everything. This is how love is: when you love someone, you always want to know more about your partner, and the more you know, the more you wish to be like him.

Unfortunately, many do not care about Jesus Christ. Money, career, an apartment, bonds, their children, going on a cruise.... all come before Jesus Christ. *Come on! Let's not exaggerate! Sunday Mass and occasional confession - is that not enough?!* What a pity ...

Others, also unfortunately, put everything upside down because they put the emphasis on self denial and think that, in order to be a good Christian, one has to suffer greatly because one has to deny oneself of many good things. Always penance, always a long face ... and so, many do not even try. Life is hard enough as it is, they reason, so why should I make it more difficult by cluttering it with all this self denial and penance.

Others approach Jesus to acquire something from him; a little consolation, a little strength, a little success, a little peace of mind, a little something ... *I can see clearly that Christ is very little known by those who think they are his friends. So much so that, since they love themselves too much, they seek in him their pleasures and consolation for themselves and not, as should those who love deeply, his bitterness and his death.*

There are *many who, although considered spiritual, are ashamed to bear witness to Christ with their deeds before men because they still suffer from self-respect."*

Saint John of the Cross argues that the key to

everything is His love for us and our love for Him. When you understand how much He cares for you and how ready He is to do everything for you, it is inevitable that in your heart is born admiration and love for Him, and you will want to please Him in all things, not through coercion but spontaneously.

In other words, it is not a question of being baptized and trying to live a good Christian life, but of letting Him build freely a relationship with you. In this light, everything becomes natural, not constrained.

But we are weak and fall easily. The seduction of this world easily mesmerizes us, allures us, and we find ourselves dragged along by the current. *Yes, I will forgive but... I don't want them to walk all over me... Yes I trust in God but... God is not going to send manna from heaven; it's better, isn't it, to insure oneself well! Children yes, of course, why not?! ... But no more than two... Nowadays children require a lot of money and attention... Yes, I do try not to get angry... but then if I do, stand out of my way!*

Yes, we are very weak. And because we are weak, we need help.

But precisely here is the gist of Christianity! We are not alone on this journey! Jesus Christ walks with us. In **The Ascent of Mount Carmel**, Saint John presents the Father addressing the soul with these words, *Jesus is every word and every answer of mine, every vision and revelation of mine, in the sense that I have already said, answered,* *shown and uncovered everything when I gave Him to you as your brother, your companion, your teacher, your redemption and your prize.*

How fortunate we are! Jesus is our brother, companion, teacher, redemption and prize. What more do we want?

Our Brother in the sense that he has linked his destiny with ours. The love of God is not vague theories or cryptic abstractions. It is a person of flesh and blood, who came into the world, lived with us, shared with us our pain and joy, and was crucified for us. Jesus is God with a human face, is God with skin on!

And this brother still walks with us on our journey. He is *the companion* of our laughter and of our tears. He is the co-partner who smiles and encourages us when he sees us lose courage, who scolds and corrects us when we do something stupid, above all, who understands us and shows compassion when we make a serious blunder. He is the friend next door.

That is why he is *our teacher* because he corrects us in order to educate us. Jesus does not spoil us but treats us as the adult persons we are. He does not want us to waste his - and our - time by treating us childishly. Our crises can be the means to enter deeply into the mystery of Christ and discover the plan of God for our lives.

He is not only our brother, our companion and our teacher, but Saint John of the Cross also calls Him *our redemption,* for He is closest to us particularly in our pain. He knows what pain is for on the cross He found Himself stripped of everything; He was left without friends, without dignity, without glory, without strength, without life... But there on the cross He loved deeply. And so, from that time on, His pain and suffering acquired an enormous value: they can ransom men.

How often have we felt ourselves crushed and broken and He has carried us on His shoulders. He showed forbearance in our weakness - once, twice, three times ... a thousand times

A girl from Baeza called Maria de la Paz stated during Saint John's beatification process that she could tell the feast of the day from his face! His face would be cheerful, let's say, at Christmas time, and sad on Good Friday. So important was Jesus Christ to him.

A final word.

Monastery of the Incarnation, Avila, some day between 1574 and 1577... Father John is praying by the window of the choir which looked down into the church. Suddenly he *sees* Christ crucified. He takes up a pen and draws rapidly, in ink, on paper what he had seen... Christ hanging on the cross looking down on the people. A standing cross, a dead body, his head suspended onward over his body, which is all projected forward, hanging only on the nails. A violent expression of suffering. The Father looking down on the son who has become *a worm of the earth* (Psalm 21), weighed down by the sins of man, suspended over the world for which he has died ...

Later he was to write that images only have meaning *if they let the soul fly from the image towards the living God.*

For him this violent expression of love is Jesus Christ. An intense, impassioned love. A love which goes beyond death.

Indeed, the Christian has every reason to rejoice.

6 - LET US FLY LIKE BIRDS

Whoever loves God loves the things God created. So it is not surprising that all the saints loved nature so much. They felt comfortable among the trees, the flowers, the sea, the blue sky, the clouds, the birds.

In the summer evenings, Father John of the Cross used to go out into the fields, lie down on the ground, looking up to the sky full of stars and spend an hour or two relishing all this beauty of God.

The sacristan of Granada left us an exquisite testimony about him: *He liked placing a flower before the Blessed Sacrament and he would always tell me how pleased God was with these trivial yet significant actions.*

One of the most attractive images that Saint John of the Cross uses to express his vision is that of the ***sparrow***. Since many of the monasteries in which he lived were surrounded by gardens, he must have often had the opportunity to admire birds.

The sparrow used to impress him for many reasons. The first feature which he remarked on was that *"this bird loves to fly very high"*. The higher the sparrow is, the happier it is. There it feels free, it is in its element, it feels sure of itself. It does not feel at ease dragging itself through the dust of the earth.

This is what the Christian can do, says the saint. The more we learn to lift up ourselves from things which pass and take no notice of them, the more free we will be and the more happily we will live. We suffer greatly because we allow our hearts to be tied to so many things. We hang on to them like an octopus and woe betide any one who tries to take them away from us. There are some who become violent if the paint of their car is scratched. Some weep inconsolably if their pet cat dies! Some spend days in a bad mood if someone tells them something which hurts them! Some get a heart attack if they get robbed in a business deal ...

We suffer because we are too much bound to things which God had provided for our use. Therefore we are not free and we cannot fly but have *to crawl on our belly all the days of our life.*

Let us take an example from the life of Saint John of the Cross. The Saint liked beautiful pictures because they helped him to pray. Once he drew a picture of a crucifix which was very impressive and which he liked so much that he put it in the breviary which he used every day for prayer. Sister Anna Maria of the monastery of the Incarnation saw it and liked it. The saint was very candid; *"Do you like it? Take it!"* ... A clear example of one who could enjoy things without tying up his heart to them.

Another incident. Before he escaped from the conventual prison of Toledo, he wished to give a small present to the friar who had looked after him, brought him food and tried to lessen the rigor of his prison. Naturally he could not tell him that he was about to escape but he wished to show him his gratitude in some way. What did he do? He had a small crucifix which was very beautiful and which Saint Teresa herself had probably given him. It was very dear to him. It was the only thing which had kept him company in those dark nights in prison. He just reached out for it and gave it to this friar. He considered it more important to make this young twenty-seven year old friar happy than to keep a crucifix cramped to his chest. A man who is detached. A free man. Hence, a happy man.

The sparrow likes to be alone. The company of other birds bothers it. If another bird comes close to it, it goes away. This is just what the Christian should learn, comments Saint John of the Cross. The more we learn to value quiet and recollection, the more we have peace of mind. The less you let people influence you, the calmer you live.

This does not mean that one should become a recluse. But it does mean that you must learn to live with people without allowing them to drag you along with their whims. Far too often we allow other people to condition us! Far too often we do not do what we think we should do but what others want us to do! There is a strong herd instinct in all of us... There are very few people who reason with their head - many just allow other people to think for them... They let their opinions be determined by the newspapers, advertisements, politicians ... always by other people.

Saint John of the Cross believed in liberty. He gives his Carmelite brothers this advice which applies also to us even though we do not live in monasteries. In a commentary which he wrote under the name of **Precautions** he declares to a friar who wishes to reach perfection quickly: *Guard yourself very carefully against thinking about what happens in the community, and even more so against speaking of it, of anything in the past or present concerning a particular religious; nothing about his character or his conduct or his deeds no matter how serious any of this seems. Do not say anything under the colour of zeal or of correcting a wrong unless at the proper time to him whom by right you ought to tell. Never be scandalized or astonished by anything you happen to see or learn of, endeavouring to preserve your soul in forgetfulness of all that. For should you desire to pay heed to things, many will seem wrong, even though you may live among angels* - he concludes ironically! - *because of your not understanding the nature of them.*

We need to learn to live with others without constantly sifting every single deed of theirs through our minds. Our thought processes are tainted and so it is so easy to pin-point the bug, the defect, the fault. We are always demanding... *my husband should have acted in this way, my wife ought to understand me better, the children ought to respect me, my work mates ought to show more collaboration ...* All these expectations cause us to suffer a great deal.

This is why Saint John of the Cross gives us this useful piece of advice. The bird prefers to be alone. He enjoys looking upwards. If only we too could learn to be less obsessed with others.

There is another quality which caught Saint John of the Cross imagination while he observed the sparrow. *The sparrow always turns its beak to the wind.* So too, the Saint comments, should the Christian act. He should learn always to turn his mind and his heart towards the Holy Spirit.

What does this mean?

Basically it means something very simple. We are not alone. When God brought us into the world, he had a plan, a beautiful dream which he is bringing about slowly. He is moving about everything for our good. Nothing happens hazardly. Nothing happens by chance. Behind every happening in our life there is the mind and the heart of Someone who loves us deeply.

We must therefore learn to discover God's hand in all the things which befall us. We must learn to be open to the inspirations of the Holy Spirit. In life there are two kinds of things which can happen to us - things which we can control : *what shall I wear? What shall I eat? To which school shall I send the children? Whom shall I marry? How many children shall I have? When shall I go out for a walk?...* And things over which we have no control - illness, death, the weather, an accident ...

What I need to learn is to accept without incrimination, indeed with joy, those things which come about and over which I have no control, because I realize that in some way, God is behind these circumstances, even if I do not like them. And, on the other hand I should learn to ask him more often what I should do with the things which I have control over.

I am planning on something? Then let me ask God if this is a good course to follow. I am going out? Let me ask Him if it is timely to leave the house now... In other words, more contact with Him. Seek his advice more often. He loves me a great deal and has a beautiful plan for me. Let us learn to always turn our mind and heart to him. Who better than Him can give us guidance to our life?!

Another thing which struck Saint John of the Cross about the sparrow is that *it sings very sweetly.* In the same way, as the Christian gradually begins to discover this enormous love of God towards him, he begins to sing praises to God.

The closer you come to God, the more you begin to view the world differently. You begin to learn how much God cares about you. Even misadventures will become in your eyes graces. Death itself starts taking on a new colour - no longer black but rather white. Illness is no longer seen as something terrible but as part of God's pedagogy to educate you. All becomes gift.

And so in your heart grievances start decreasing and gratitude starts rising. You become less gripy and more appreciative. In your heart music begins to flow. A beautiful hymn of thanksgiving.

The last trait Saint John notices about the sparrow is that *it does not have a single colour.* It has all the colours. In the same way, the more the Christian grows in the love of God, the less he allows others to sway him. Only one thing becomes important to him and that is the will of God, since he realizes that only here lies heaven

After his meeting with the Samaritan woman, Jesus Christ himself told his apostles that his only food was to do the will of his Father. This was the bread which sustained him. This was the bread which replenished him. The Christian too - even if a Gethsemane looms before him, even if the cross appears before him - knows that it is there that he will be happy, not when he does what he himself wants.

God's pedagogy in this respect is impressive. He gradually guides us from the sweetness of our early fervour, where our spiritual satisfaction is our main concern, to true love where the important thing becomes His satisfaction!

Let us hear one of John's most beautiful pages. *When a soul first turns to God with determination, God usually feeds her and nurtures her as a good mother does with her young son - she draws him to her breast, feeds him with good milk, gives him fine and delicate food, holds him in her arms, and makes much of him. But once the boy begins to grow, the mother gradually begins to cuddle him less and hiding her tender love, she puts bitter herbs on her breast, and puts the child down from her arms and teaches him to walk on his two feet until the child, losing what made him a child, is given better and more important things.*

The grace of God is like this tender mother. It acts in the same way with the soul... Yes, indeed, our mission is to fly... *Even youths grow tired and weary, and young men stumble and fall; but those who hope in the Lord will renew their strength. They will soar on wings like eagles; they will run and not grow weary, they will walk and not be faint,* as the Prophet says. It is possible with Him!

7 - Mary, the humble Virgin of Nazareth

Woman is precious in the life of man. Everybody needs a mother who understands him and cares for him. As our mother gave us our body and to a great extent formed our character, so in in our faith we have a mother who bore us into our new life. Mary climbed up Mount Calvary with her only Son and came down with all of us as her children. This is why it is inevitable that the true Christian has a true bond with Mary.

Father John of the Cross loved Our Lady very deeply. And he had good reason, for she loved him very dearly.

It was she, *a very beautiful woman,* who saved him on two occasions when he, a mischievous little boy, fell, once into a pool, another time into a well.

These are the facts. He was five or six years old. The little boy went to play with some friends near a pool at Fontiveros. They were standing at the edge of the pool trying to bounce pieces of wood along the waters surface by throwing them with all their might and then trying to catch them as they came out of the water. John slipped and fell into the water. He surfaced but went under water again. He himself recounted later that he saw *a beautiful woman who asked me to give her my hand while she stretched out her hand to me.* But he would not hold her hands because he was afraid he would dirty them! Meanwhile a farmer arrived who held out a rod to the little boy so that he could catch on to it and then pulled him gently to the shore.

When he was still in the *De los doctrinos* College he had a similar adventure. This time a companion pushed him and he fell into a well which was situated in the courtyard of one of the hospitals. Some of the kids ran away while others began calling for help. A few adults came to the rescue and were surprised to find him floating in the water. *I have not drowned. Our Lady saved me. Throw down a rope so that I can tie myself to it and then you can pull me up.*

True stories? Fantasy? Many people mentioned these two incidents at his beatification process. Mary knows how to protect her children; who knows, when all will be revealed, how many times we will discover that Mary has saved us from drowning! All kinds of drowning!

It was Mary who, in the Church of Saint Anna in Medina del Campo, inspired him to enter her Order - the Carmelite Order. The Carmelite Order owes its origin to a few hermits who lived on Mount Carmel near Haifa. There the prophet Elijah had a dramatic confrontation with the prophets of Baal.

Carmel is a range of beautiful hills covered in greenery. It was an ideal place for these men to spend their lives interceding with the Lord for mankind. There they built a small chapel which they dedicated to Our Lady and which gave a Marian dimension to their whole spirituality. They realized early in their history how strongly Jesus is bound to Mary.

Saint Teresa of Jesus, when trying to encourage him to join her in founding the male Discalced Carmel, used his love of Our Lady to persuade him not to think of joining other congregations. Carmel is totally Marian. *Why go seeking somewhere else when you have everything you need in your own home?* she asserted.

Since we know that nothing happens by chance in the life of the Christian, it is significant that it was on the eve of the feast of the Assumption that he managed to escape from the prison of Toledo, where he had been imprisoned for eight and a half months. Indeed it was the fact that he had been denied permission to say mass on that Solemnity - a feast very dear to his heart - which prompted him to take the risk of escaping.

His companions, the friars, tell us that often, during his long journeys, he would sing hymns to Our Lady. On his death bed, when he heard the bells ringing for Matins, he told the friars who were beside his bed: *If God wants, tonight I will sing Matins with the Virgin Mary"* and so it was, for at midnight, on the 14th of December 1591 he passed to the true life. It was a ... Saturday!

Yes, he loved Mary deeply. So much so that on the few occasions that he mentions her in his writings, he always uses delightful words about her. He does not mention her often in his writings because he did not wish to repeat what has already been said by others. Furthermore, Mary is such a beautiful and delicate person that too many words can easily cloud her beauty. Before beauty, the less said, the better. One can perhaps utter some verses:

*Then he called
the Archangel Gabriel
And sent him
to the Virgin Mary.*

*At whose consent
the mystery was wrought,
In whom the Trinity
 clothed the Word with flesh.*

*And though Three work this
It is wrought in the One
and the Word lived incarnate
in the womb of Mary.*

And He who had only a Father
 now has a mother too
But she was not like others
who conceive by man.

From her own flesh
He received His flesh,
so He is called
son of God and of man.

The poem he wrote about Christmas contains only four lines, but here again one can feel the intensity of the heart of this Saint:

The Virgin, weighed
with the Word of God
comes down the road;
if only you shelter her.

In the **Ascent of Mount Carmel** he affirms that Mary never had anything or anyone imprinted or engraved in her mind: it was always the Holy Spirit who guided her. This is why she was so sure in her journey. If only we learn this secret from her... we would stagger less in life!!

Far too often we feel depressed in life because we fill our imagination with trivialities and stupidities. We live in a society in which it is not the content which is important but the ability to sell it!   Commercials have taken over control of our lives and we find ourselves puppets in the hands of these money-grabbers. They lead us where they want to. They think for us. They make us spend our money as it suits them. We finish up buying many superfluous things. They force us to yearn and crave for so many futile commodities.

We undergo the same blizzard in our affections. Because of our thirst to be loved we live a carnival all the year long! We act not as we want to act but as others want us to react. We smile when we feel like crying and we cry when we feel like laughing. Always wearing masks ... efficiency, laughter, good-manners, propriety... Our minds and hearts are always concerned about what others think of us, whether others really love us.

This is why Mary fascinated him. And she can fascinate us as well. In her he sees a woman who let the Holy Spirit guide her. The Holy Spirit is a spirit of consolation and prudence. A Spirit of love and wisdom. He knows which way to guide us. His ways are always excellent, for He loves us with an eternal love.

In the **Living Flame of Love**, he clarifies an important truth when he says that Mary had the Spirit of God so close to her that He overshadowed her.

To overshadow someone means to shelter and favour someone, because when we say that one is overshadowed by someone, we mean that, that person is very close to you, to give you the favours you need and to protect you. Therefore the grace which God gave to Mary when she gave birth to the Son of God was described by the angel Gabriel as the shadow of the Holy Spirit: 'The Holy Spirit shall come upon thee and the power of the most High shall overshadow thee.'

Radiance in life lies in being near the one who loves you. Unfortunately many of us have lived a religion which relied excessively on the fear of possible punishment. The law used to, and still does, prevail in our churches.

Mary allowed the Spirit to be near her to shield her always from the attacks of the evil one and at the same time to warm her with his blazing fire.

In the **Spiritual Canticle,** John takes the example of Mary, who at the marriage of Cana, so graciously does not hustle Jesus because the couple have no wine, but she simply presents their situation before her son Jesus ... and leaves everything in His hands! We too, says Saint John of the Cross, should never try to force God to give in to our wishes. Prayer should change us not God!

He who loves does not keep worrying and asking for his needs and wants, but simply shows his needs. This is what the Virgin did at the marriage in Cana of Galilee when, without making any demands, she said, 'they have no wine' ...

Christian prayer, this *"dichosa ventura" (i.e. marvelous adventure),* as Saint John of the Cross used to call it, is totally different from the prayer of the religious man. The pious man, when threatened by some illness or misadventure moans to God to deliver him from it. He divides life into good things and bad things, boons and troubles. Boons are those things which agree with his ideas of happiness, while troubles are those things which do not agree with his idea.

The Christian knows that since he has an Abba, a

Father in heaven, everything must be good. All works for his good ... even illness and death. Therefore he does not ask God to change history in his favour because he knows already that history is always in his favour! Instead he approaches God to show him his situation, to open his heart to Him, to express to God how difficult it is for him to accept these circumstances and to ask God to help him accept the will of the Father. It is the prayer of a friend who approaches his friend to cry and laugh with him, it is the prayer of a child who leaps on to his Father's lap... *He who is little, let him come to me!* - says the Word.

Mary realized the problems that arose at the wedding and left everything in the hands of Jesus. She was convinced that He knew better than she what He had to do.

Later in the same book, when commenting on the spiritual marriage between God and man, John presents Mary as an example. It is possible to reach such an intimate union with Jesus. But there is one path. The very path which Bin Sirach mentions: *My son, if you want to serve the Lord prepare yourself for trials"* The same path the Master walked before and for us - the path of the cross. The life of Mary also, says this friar, was marked by a lot of grief. The cross appeared often in her life. She was even forced to go into exile in a foreign land with her young son. But she continued believing that God loved her. She never doubted His love. She kept seeing the light even in the dark of night.

We can condense the focus of the Virgin of Nazareth in two words: she was a servant - *He has looked with favour on his lowly servant* and a lover. A servant of God. A lover of God.

This is why Saint John of the Cross can sing in the **Prayer of the Enamoured Soul**: *All is mine, even the Mother of God is mine.* Indeed Mary is ours. Our lives would be more beautiful if we learn to appreciate this woman.

In **Romances** 8 and 9, where he is talking about the plan of salvation which God has for man, the Saint shows Mary's wonder in front of the lofty mystery which is taking place before her eyes. Why do we not wonder at this same mystery which is blossoming in front of our eyes?

To a girl from Narros del Castillo, who wished to join the Carmelite Nuns in Madrid, John gave her this advice: *Pray a great deal, leave everything in the hands of God, and and as your advocate take Our Lady Mary and also Saint Joseph.*
A good recommendation, don't you think?!

8 - The art of loving

The 7th December was Saturday, the eve of the feast of the Immaculate Conception. His temperature was very high, and the colour of the pus coming out of the wounds covering his body had changed colour. The doctor, Ambrosio de Villareal looked worried. *What day is today?* the sick man asked. *Blessed are you, Our Lady, you who want me to leave this life on your day - Saturday.* His companions asked themselves whether he would die next Saturday?

Two days later Father Alonso de la Madre de Dios gave him the news that the doctor expected him to die soon. *I rejoiced when they said: 'let us go to God's house!' After hearing this good news I no longer feel the pain.* His heart was already in heaven. Now it was simply a question of dragging his body there also. The beloved was there *on the other side.*

On Friday 13th, feast of Saint Lucy, the ill man asked his nurse, Fra Diego, if he was feeling sad that he was dying. *I said yes,* Fra Diego remarked later, *but I leave everything in the hands of God and hope always that God's will be done.* Father John was pleased with this answer. He then asked the brother to call the prior Francisco Crisostomo and *with great humility he asked his pardon for all his shortcomings and the trouble he had caused the prior because of his illness. He asked the prior to ensure that he would be buried in the poor habit of Our Lady which he always wore.* He remained a son of Mary to the end.

The provincial Father Anton de Jesus (Heredia) came to visit him and tried to encourage him and remind him of how they much they had suffered at the beginning of the Reform. Fray John does not wish to be reminded ...

Apparently he is calm. But on the inside, a whole struggle is going on. It is not an easy death: *I assure you,* he says to Father Augustine at eight o'clock in the evening, *that there is nothing in my life which is not indicting me now!* There is a mixture of emotions: joy, courage, fear, contrition, hope ...

At eleven o'clock, he asks the Prior to bring him the Blessed Sacrament so that he can look at it for the last time with his bodily eyes. At eleven thirty, when the Prior starts reading the prayers of the Ritual for the dead, Fray John stops him and says: *Father, read me the Song of Songs. What precious pearls!!* - he begins to murmur while listening to those passionate and fiery words.

As the bells start ringing midnight, he kisses the cross which he holds in his hands: *Into your hands O Lord, I commend my spirit* and he closes his eyes. The next time he opens them again he is already contemplating eternity. It was the first minute of Saturday 14th December 1591.

The name of this sick friar is Father John of the Cross. He was forty nine years old.

He had arrived at this monastery of San Miguel in Ubeda three months earlier from Penuela, because a small abscess on his right leg had developed into an ugly tumor which slowly spread over all his limbs and also through his shoulders. The Prior of the house in Ubeda did not welcome him favourably. He gave him the worst room, he constantly complained about the cost of the medicine that they had to disburse because of his illness, he used to make John attend choir even when he was very weak because of his high fever, he created many difficulties in giving out permission for lay people and friars to visit him in his room...

The way he lived his last week, totally bedridden, give us an insight into his maturity. His strong altruism shines forth clearly. He did not complain against the Prior, but loved him and asked his forgiveness. He was able to go beyond the facade and respect even the one who was treating him badly. The Christian is always aware that the other is in pain. He knows that the other is full of internal hurts which are oozing a lot of pus, and so he knows how to be compassionate. The Christian believes all, excuses all and endures all.

Like the Master.

Saint John of the Cross had drunk this altruism from his mother. It was she who had taught him that in life there is more joy in giving than in receiving. It is impressive how this poor woman never closed herself in her shell even when the ones who were supposed to help her, after her husband's death, slammed the door in her face and the face of her children. Love, this kind of love will conquer the world.

Faith and love are like two children who lead a blind man. They lead you through paths you do not know, until you reach the hiding place of God. For faith is like the limbs that take the soul to God, and love is the guide which leads it.

As a young fifteen year old boy, he used to work willingly in the *De las bubas* hospital as a nurse among the patients with infectious diseases.

Later he was able to form deep friendships with many nuns and lay people. He remained always a great friend of his brother Francis, even when their lives took different directions. Mind you, his character was not the extrovert type, the 'hale fellow well met' kind but his friendships were strong and true.

His companion who knew him very well tells us a very beautiful story. A rich lady from Avila, beautiful and a music-lover had a deep problem with her rage: she used to suffer from serious tantrums to such an extent that quite often she would finish up smashing all that she found before her. She was advised to go to confession to Father John. *No way!* she answered! *He is too saintly for my tastes,* she always added. *If I tell him something, he will snap at me.* Anyway, finally she was convinced to go and speak to him. He picked up immediately the fear of this lady and so, to reassure her, he welcomed her by saying: *The holier a confessor is, the more he is compassionate and the less easily he is scandalized!* After her confession, this lady told Sister Anna Maria that her greatest penance was the effort to go over to see him, because afterwards everything became easy. Her life changed.

His provincial Father Gabriel commented after his death: *His writings are good, but he is a saint because he himself was so good with everybody.*

The closer one comes to God, the more one understands others. And the more one sees God in them. And the happier one is!

Father Francis of the Mother of God, a Discalced Carmelite friar, a companion of Saint John of the Cross, left us this beautiful testimony about him. He tells that Father John used always to tell his friars that wherever they are they must never get tired of doing good to others ; in this simple way they display that they are children of God. *Offend nobody,* he would say, *neither by words nor by actions, and know that if we do not pay attention to this, we will be doing more harm to ourselves than to others!*

Another friar, Luis de San Angel would often see him listening to and consoling scrupulous people that all others would avoid because they were so nerve-wracking. Father John used to listen to them and console them even if he had a lot of work to do as superior of the house.

A well known story is that on one occasion, while hearing confession, he realized that one particular nun had a badly torn habit. He was so touched that he went himself begging for money so that he could have another habit made for her.

Among the fourteen sentences which Father Andrew of the Incarnation collected from the Saint's mouth, we find this jewel: *He is meek who is able to have patience with his brother and also patience with himself.*

On another occasion he stated that *the soul that is full of love is sweet, tranquil, humble and full of patience.*

One favourite sentence of his was this: *A pure and complete deed made with a pure heart for the love of God prepares a whole kingdom for him who does it.*

One more story shows the sensitivity of the saint towards others, even towards those who were outside his immediate circle. He was taking his recreation with his companions in Granada. At a certain moment he took a handful of gravel and started dividing the stones, placing some on one side and some on the other. Then he picked up one small pebble and put it to one side and kept looking at it. When his companions saw him so thoughtful they asked him what had happened. He told them:*I am thinking how little the Lord is known in this world. Look, in all these parts of the world , they have not heard of Him yet. They have only heard of him in this little portion ... and even here few are the chosen ones.*

Let us not forget that at that time Christopher Columbus had just discovered America and many of the friends of Saint John of the Cross and relatives of the friars were in America as *conquistadores*. Therefore the missionary issue necessarily was on the mind of Saint John of the Cross.

At the end of his life there was even the possibility that he should go to Mexico. We all know that there are three groups of Christians in the world: those who bury their heads in the sand and ignore what's happening, those who sit in the grandstand and watch things happen, and those who roll up their sleeves and make things happen. This saint rolled up his sleeves and did something. He realized that Jesus Christ gives meaning to life, and offers a solution to the problems which trouble mankind.

Therefore his heart was inflamed with the wish to spread the good news.

Father Eliseus of the Martyrs, one of the companions of Saint John of the Cross, wrote this about him after the saint's death: *John of the Cross, when expounding the words of Christ 'do you not know that I must be about my father's business?' told us that the business of the Father is the redemption of the world and the good of souls. He reminded us of the words of Saint Dionysus who said that among the good deeds he could do, the most beautiful is to work with God to save souls ... because thus we would be doing something which truly pleases God.*

Today we would call it zeal for evangelization.

Love was the motor of his life. The more one is acquainted with God, the more one feels for men and the more one wishes them to enjoy the same joy and love which only God can give. May all of us become not only lovers but also teachers in the art of loving - *maestras de amar.*

9 -THE OPTIMISM OF GOD

Father John of the Cross was thirty years old when he had a colourful experience. A beautiful girl from a rich family fell head over heels in love with him. She would go to see him frequently on one pretext or another, but she was unable to attract his attention. Therefore, she decided to dare more! One evening she sneaked into the room in which he lived. Father John was eating alone. He was amazed when he saw her there, standing, in front of him. He did not get indignant or scold her or chase her away. No, he simply spoke to her gently and after a while, she burst into tears and left. Saints have a lot of charm and grace. They have deep insights in human nature.

After all, even saints have their temptations. Without temptations no one can be saved.

We also have our difficult moments in life, because Satan always tries to put his foot in to ruin our day. Sometimes it is the wife, sometimes the husband, sometimes the children, sometimes our work mates, sometimes it is a car tyre puncture ... apparently something must happen every single day to mar our happiness.

Once Saint John of the Cross summarized the secret of perfection in four short phrases:

To forget the created.
Always remember the creator.
Guard always the interior life.
Always love the Beloved.

The pretty girl wanted to embrace Father John. He showed her that it is better to embrace God

Once, during a conference he was giving to the nuns, Maria de la Cruz, a Carmelite nun, asked the saint whether she could go and drink some water. His answer was indeed timely: *Yes go and drink, but drink God as well!!*

Drink God. In other words, allow God to refresh you, let him enter and circulate in your veins, let God fill you interiorly.

God is wholesome water. In the **Spiritual Canticle**, John compares God to a river. A river of joy. A river of living water. A river which cleanses the soul. With my mind I can drink the wisdom of God and with my heart I can drink the sweetest love of God.

How wonderful is God who is able to fill us with himself. How good He is who allows himself to be enticed by our love.

God is the kind of person who can only be charmed by love. When He finds someone who loves Him, He gets confused! And He does everything possible to stay with the person who loves him. In his book **The Ascent of Mount Carmel** John repeats again what he has already explained in the Canticle:

The Lord is so made that, if one approaches Him with good manners and according to His nature, one can do whatever one wants with Him; but if one approaches Him for one's own personal interest, there is no point in even talking to Him!!

Even God has his own style in making relationships! He is big hearted, and when He sees someone who truly loves Him, He immediately approaches him.

Father John of the Cross used to enjoy writing short sentences which he called **Sayings of Light and Love**.[17] These are short sayings which trigger consideration, and, above all, help one to come closer to God. The first saying is indeed powerful. It says:

The Lord has always revealed to men the treasure of His wisdom and His Spirit, but now that the face of evil bares itself, so does the Lord bare His treasures even more.

In other words, it is true that evil exists. It is true that evil apparently is becoming always more arrogant, aggressive and triumphant. All of us suffer the temptation of thinking that in life it is better not to mind anything except our own interests. It is not the first time that we tried to do someone a good turn and have been repaid with evil.

But evil never has the last word. Jesus Christ has come and fought a harsh battle against evil. And evil battered Him. It even killed him. Apparently everything was annihilated. Once again evil seemingly had the last laugh! But three days later a man came out of the cemetery. Victorious. Jesus Christ rose from the dead. Triumphant over all that shackles man and prevents him from being free. Even death has been conquered!

And from that day onwards, whosoever unites himself to Christ receives a guarantee that there is nothing that can overcome him. *Wickedness is always weakness,* comments the saint. But *the soul united with Christ is like a lion, courageous and strong. Therefore, the devils,* continues the saint, *do not even dare to fight with the soul, because they are terrified the moment they see her.*

The devil is scared of the man who is united with Jesus Christ. Alone we are worthless, but with Him we can win every battle.

Very often we suffer in life because we look at everything through dark glasses. We fix our attention on gloom. We see the sombre aspects of our life. We just see the defects in others. It is as if God has made a mess of everything!

This pessimism takes our breath away. Every hurdle is a stepping stone. Life is like a piano with both black and white notes; if one plays both properly, beautiful music come out. We need new eyes to see that in life there is nothing but graces. All is beautiful for he who can see. All is free gift.

Saint John of the Cross used to love repeating *through hope one acquires that which one longs for.* He wrote these words to a nun:

You already know, daughter, the trials we are now suffering. Do not worry. God permits them for the glory of his elect. In silence and in hope shall our strength be.

Indeed every affliction God sends is positive. God is able to turn everything to our advantage. Everything. The important thing in life is to learn to accept and to wait. After the night, comes the dawn. Always.

But how am I to realize this? How can I learn to see beauty in everything? How am I to learn not to complain so much? Saint John of the Cross believes that the key to everything lies in how much you and I are willing to let God penetrate to the very marrow of our lives.

To explain this he uses a simple example. He notices that when the sun shines on a window, if the window is dirty, it cannot light the room; but if the window panes are clean, the rays of the sun can penetrate the glass and fill the room with light; indeed, the very glass panes become light.

It is very similar with the soul, comments the saint. God is always emitting his rays of light upon us; we are like the window panes. If we are clean and without stain, then we too begin to shine like God. We become like God. In other words, if we are able to let go of the many trivialities which choke the stomach of our soul, God can fill us and sustain us. We ourselves become light. So we will be able to enlighten others.

A nun on the missions was walking down the street when she saw a poor old man who was dying all alone on the edge of the road. She managed to drag him to her convent. She washed him, fed him, put him to bed, and started conversing with him. A little while before he closed his eyes to open them in eternity, she asked him if he believed in God, and he whispered with a twinkle in his eyes and a smile in his face: *Yes, now I believe in God because I have seen you.*

This is what God does if we let Him. He changes us into Himself and so we can change others. We can warm others with the same fondness that God has warmed us.

For indeed, to end with the words of the saint, *in the evening, we will be examined in love. Therefore learn to love God as he wishes to be loved.*

10 - A NIGHT SHINING AS BRIGHTLY AS THE DAY

I believe it was Napoleon who was once on a Mediterranean terrace with a companion. It was a beautiful night full of stars and Napoleon asked his friend: *Can you see the stars?* The other one, who had very poor eyesight answered *No.* Then Napoleon declared: *This is the difference between you and me; I can see the stars and you cannot.*

The Christian is one who sees the stars; in other words he has a vision, an aim in life. He knows that life makes sense because heaven exists, because everything is a masterpiece of art made by His Father who is in heaven and on earth.

He looks around him and is radiant because everything reminds him of his beloved. If nature - the trees, the wind, the sea, the fields, the flowers - is so beautiful, how much more beautiful must be He who made them and who keeps them alive?

Once Father John of the Cross asked me on what I was meditating, stated a Carmelite nun from Beas, Suor Francesca de la Madre de Dios. *I answered him that I was contemplating the beauty of God. The saint was elated with this answer and for many days he told us beautiful and exalted things about the beauty of God which amazed us all.*

This beauty is God. But man does not discover this at once. There is a process which takes time. There is a way which one must walk gradually and with much patience.

One is not born a Christian. One *becomes* a Christian.

The word of God speaks repeatedly of the journey which the people of God made through the desert. This is the same journey which we too must make. Often during this journey pain appears, suffering breaks out, night comes forth.

The scripture calls this way a desert, because the people of God made the journey precisely through a desert. A desert full of sand ... hot and sunny during the day, cold and moonlit during the night. This is a place where like it or not you have to divest yourself of everything.

But this is also a place where God purifies and clarifies ideas. A place where God makes you free. Because here you are taught to walk not according to your feelings or your logical thoughts, but according to His feelings and thoughts. The desert is a place where God educates you, where he leads you to the promised land.

This journey through the desert is what Saint John of the Cross calls the *night.* A dark night. It is night because in it one must strip oneself bare of everything; one has to divest oneself from all the unnecessary and ill-suited attachments that man has in the world : a night for the senses of man.

It is a night because one must walk in the dark... The journey is a journey in faith where man must learn to walk trusting ONLY on naked faith: for the mind which always seeks to understand everything, this is indeed a dark night.

It is a night because we are moving towards God, our goal, who is darkness in our eyes - when we look towards the sun, its strong light dazzles our eyes...

Saint John of the Cross loved the night a great deal. Quite often, after Compline, his companions in the Carmel of Andalucia would find him at the window, looking out into the night at the stars. Saint Teresa herself tells us in her book **The Foundations** that the first friars of Duruelo used to spend whole nights between matins and morning prayer in silence.

But not all nights are the same! There is the night full of freshness and breeze at sundown, when all the lights of the day are extinguished slowly. There is the pitch-black night at midnight especially on a moon less night. There is the night which gradually gives way to the light of dawn ...

The night may give you rest and solace, but it may frighten and intimidate you. Whoever has spent a night awake in bed, sick with fever, knows what this means!

Like the desert, the night is a space where you are alone with yourself. You only have yourself. And it not always comfortable to be alone...

But this night is very important. *He who seeks his satisfaction in everything no longer keeps himself empty so that God might fill him with His ineffable delight. Thus just as he goes to God so does he return, for his hands are encumbered and cannot receive what God is giving. May God deliver us from these evil obstacles which hinder such sweet and delightful freedom,* John wrote to the nuns of Beas.

The fruit of the night are enormous. They are liberty, happiness and love. *The soul now comes to resemble one who has been delivered from chains and brought out of a dark prison so that she can now enjoy space and freedom* ... The freedom she enjoys *is a foretaste of the great joy to which she aspires.* It is a night which purifies the soul so that *she is able to communicate freely with the wisdom of God.*

Everybody must pass through this night because this is the only way that God has to refine us and raise us up to Him. *Whoever loves discipline loves learning, but whoever hates chastisement is senseless* says the Word of God. What is better than the Lord's discipline? Is it not better that *He* chastises us than ...

This night is the mystery of Easter. The passage from

death to life. Always on an ever deeper and more intense level.

But in reality what is this night? John speaks of two kinds of night -the active night and the passive night. *The active night* means the effort I do to purify myself once I become aware that I cannot continue the drudgery of my present existence. Once I realize how much God loved me and has forgiven me, I commit myself not to keep on living a life of mediocrity, constantly making compromises with everything. *The passive night* is the suffering and trials which the Lord sends me without consulting me to free me. It is the Lord who sends them ...

Here is a useful advice on the active night. John well knows that *as an act of virtue brings about and inflames in the soul sweetness, peace, consolation, light , purity and strength, so any bad tendency brings about suffering, trouble, tiredness blindness and weakness.*

This is why John comes out with phrases which sound alien to our mushy sensibility. But if one understands them, they open a way of enormous liberty.

Do not try to find what is easier, but choose always the most difficult. Not what gives you most enjoyment, but what you most dislike. Not what gives you the most pleasure, but what you like least. Not what gives you rest but what tires you most. Not what gives you consolation but that in which there is no consolation. Not the greatest but the least. Not the highest and finest, but the lowest and least esteemed. Not what you long for but what has no attraction. Never seek the best of the things of the world but the worst. In this way try to enter emptiness, poverty and total denial of all the things of this world for the love of Christ.

Words which perhaps leave you breathless when you hear them. But these words have a lot of psychological sense. John believed that if you chose of your own free will, to give up pleasure, you will enjoy life more. You will be more free.

In what sense? In the sense that often we let our inclinations and our instincts lead us. And this leads us into a lot of trouble. I know I had better not say such and such a comment. I know I should not eat that food. I know I should sleep longer hours. But my inclinations many times force me to do things which ruin my health and my life.

Far too often in life, we find ourselves pulled hither and thither by our shallow tendencies. Saint John call these inclinations *appetites.*

These appetites, as Saint John of the Cross analyzes so well in his famous book **The Ascent of Mount Carmel** not only tire man out but wear him out, blind him, weaken him and dirty his soul. Man becomes like a cracked cup which is never filled no matter how much water you pour into it. This is our daily experience; despite all our endeavors to satisfy ourselves, we always feel more empty, more disillusioned, more stressed.

Saint John of the Cross believed that if I am willing from time to time to detach myself from the pleasure which my senses give me, it will be easier for me to reason with my mind (and not with my instinct) and so I will be more free to do what is truly right for me. Man becomes more balanced.

But this is not an empty psychological exercise . This is an exercise of love. When one falls in love, one tries to please his beloved. When you love, you enjoy making up secrets between you and your partner. The Christian gradually learns to focus all his energy and all his pleasure on the only One who loves him. Detachment makes sense because it is the other side of the coin of love.

But there is another more important night - the passive night. A situation happens to you which forces you to put many question marks on your life - on the meaning of all that you do and live. In reality, this night has many names. It could be an illness, an accident, an interior dryness, a setback at work or in the family, an injustice you have suffered without deserving it. It is always a situation where you feel as if everything around you is falling apart and vanishing. A situation of weakness. A limit-situation. Often a situation of pain and anguish.

Here comes out with power the really divine science of Saint John of the Cross. He penetrates the mystery of the night. And he finds a profound logic. He himself had suffered many nights in his life - the death of his father and his older brother when he was a little boy, the humiliation of having to beg for a living when he was an adolescent, the unjust imprisonment for nine months which he suffered at the age of thirty-five, the calumnies which were invented about him just a year before he died.

In this pain, he discovered something awesome. Night is not a calamity, pain is not a defeat. On the contrary, night can be a grace, pain may become a means of salvation:

> *O guiding night!*
> *O night more lovely than the dawn!*
> *O night that has united*
> *the lover with his beloved*
> *transforming the beloved in her lover.*

John believes that the night is necessary. Suffering is indispensable. It is absolutely essential to surrender all things in order to achieve intimacy with Him. And since we are not capable of doing this, God brings about this miracle of love Himself; since we are incapable of detaching ourselves, He does the disconnection!

This is similar to when one is ill. What do the nurses do? They keep the patient in bed, warm, sometimes even in the dark, they try to eliminate all noises and draught, they give him special food which often is insipid but full of vitamins and nourishment ... all this for the good of the sick person. The patient, if he is intelligent does not find it difficult to accept being denied of so many things so that he may recover. Here the case is the same... except that the disease is deep within, and therefore needs a more vigorous treatment!

The night may become a bed of love where you unite and become one with your Beloved. Suffering may marry you to Jesus Christ!

I abandoned and forgot myself,
Laying my face on my Beloved;
All things ceased; I went out from myself,
leaving my cares
forgotten among the lilies.

It is not surprising that he gives this advice:

When something which troubles you or something you
do not like happens to you, look at Christ crucified and
keep silent. Live in faith and through hope, even if you are
in the darkness, because just in these things God comes
to the aid of the soul .

Do not complain. Do not try to distract yourself. Do
not bemoan yourself. But embrace the cross and you will
start cherishing life.

Life taught John this precious lesson through many
experiences. Let us mention one night in his life - an
important night.

He was forty six years old when in a General Chapter,
that is a general meeting of the Friars, his colleagues did
not elect him to any office. He did not agree with their
policies so they put him aside. Men have always been the
same! What was worse was that the man who replaced
him, a young thirty year old friar called Diego Evangelista,
began a campaign of calumnies and lies about him. Stories
were spread about nuns and relationships and all sorts of
stupid things.

The next six months were indeed hard ones for John. We know of two occasions when he cried; once when he was talking to a nun in Malagon and once in Toledo when he was returning from the chapter of Madrid. Both occasions were in this period of his life.

Meanwhile his health was deteriorating rapidly because of the the tumor in his leg which was infecting all his body.

This was indeed a dark night for John. Physical pain. Anguish caused by the lack of comprehension and even wickedness of his fellow religious.

How did he react? Did he become angry? Or grumble? Or fight for his rights? Or become embittered? Or spend his times bemoaning his fate?

We know his reaction from a letter - one of the few extant ones, since, in order to avoid increasing the trouble which was looming around him, he insisted on having all his letters destroyed. It is a letter which he wrote to one of the nuns in whom he had most trust - Anna de Jesus.

Thank you very much for your letter; this puts me under greater obligation than before. If things did not turn out as you desired, you ought rather to be consoled and thank God profusely. Since His Divine Majesty has so arranged matters, it is what most suits everyone. All that remains for us is to accept it willingly so that once we believe He has arranged this, we may show it by our actions. Things that do not please us seem to be evil and harmful, however good and fitting they may be."

On another occasion he had written - while talking with the friars and nuns - that if we are unable to be satisfied with what God sends us on earth, we will not even be happy in heaven! Even there we would find things to complain about!!

During this same period, he wrote another letter to the mother of Sister Anna - a married woman who, after the death of her husband, became a Carmelite nun and was living in the same monastery as her daughter. His words show a very mature and practical attitude when faced with this debacle.

Do not let what is happening to me, daughter, cause you any grief, for it does not cause me any. What greatly grieves me is that he who is not at fault is being blamed. Men do these things, but God knows what is suitable for us, and arranges things for our good. Think of nothing else but that God orders all, and where there is no love, put love, and you will draw out love.

These are simple principles. Basic principles. Principles which can change a life. Let us repeat them ...

When something which troubles you or something you do not like, comes about, look at Christ crucified and keep silent.

These things are not done by men but by God Himself. He knows what we most need and disposes of our lives for our own good.

Think of nothing else but that God ordains all and where there is no love, put love and you will draw out love.

When you begin to see things in this way, the darkness becomes light, and the troubles and problems of life will not crush you, but on the contrary, they will build you up to ... eternal life.

11 - LET US LEARN TO HIDE

Yekiel, the grandson of Rabbi Baruk was playing hide and seek with his friend. He found a good hiding place and waited for his companion to find him. But he waited in vain. He left his hiding place and not finding his companion around, he realized that the other had not even tried to look for him! He took it so badly that he started crying and went over to his grandfather whining about his companion, who did not look for him when he had hidden himself so well. His grandfather's eyes also started filling with tears as he began to murmur to himself:*This is just what God says: I hide myself and nobody comes to seek me...*

Yes, God suffers because few people bother to seek him with all their heart. Indeed, *You are a hidden God, O God and Savior of Israel"* says the prophet Isaiah. He hides and he hides himself well. And apparently few are the ones who bother to waste their time looking for him.

Our God is a God who is enamoured of men. And being the kind of lover He is, He enjoys playing with us. He loves playing hide and seek. He hides so that we can go out and look for Him. It is a game of love. A beautiful game. Indeed, since He is not only a lover but also a great artist, He can hide Himself really well.

He uses a tempting manouver. First He lets you fall madly in love with Him, first He gives you a taste of how delightful it is to stay with him, and then ... He disappears.

The Spiritual Canticle starts just like this ... with the sigh coming out of a soul wounded with love:

Where have you hidden?
Beloved, and left me moaning?
You fled like the stag
After wounding me;
I went out calling You, and You were gone.

He has gone and hidden himself.

Who knows how many times you too, in a difficult moment of your life, or during the drudgery of housework at home or the pressures at the office or after a serious conflict with the children, you felt like talking to God, you felt the need of someone who understands and cares for you, someone who could give you courage , and you turned to God .. and did not find Him. Apparently He had disappeared, he had concealed himself. He is everywhere, and yet He is nowhere ...

Even when He came into the world, many did not even notice him. They thought He was an ordinary man, indeed there were even some who labeled him possessed by the devil, a glutton, a madman. Only the poor, the sick, the sinners recognized Him. I wonder, what does this mean?

Now too He hides.

He hides in the Eucharist. The Curè of Ars once said, pointing at the tabernacle: *Our Lord is there hidden, waiting for us to go and visit Him and speak to Him. Look how good He is. He adapts Himself to our weakness; if He appeared to us in His glory, none of us would dare to approach Him ...*

He hides in His Word, in the events which happen, in the humdrum events of our everyday lives. He hides in our neighbor: the other, our husband, our wife, my colleagues at work are the hidden God...

Often, far too often, we are not aware of this. Things happen to us and we do not see God anywhere. We come face to face with other people and it never occurs to us that they are Christ. It is not by chance that the Gospel speaks so often about blind men - people who see nothing but the dark.

We need different glasses, a more penetrating gaze in order for us to recognize Him.

Saint John of the Cross helps us to acquire this new outlook. He teaches us to see in the dark. Otherwise, if we always react simply according to outward appearances, we shall suffer greatly. The blind man easily bumps himself and gets hurt.

The Christian is the person who gradually acquires

the eyes of Jesus Christ. He begins to see people and things as God sees them. This is what the Saint believes.

In skillful verses, Saint John of the Cross expresses himself thus - these are rich and dense verses:

O spring like crystal
If only, on your silvered -over face,
You would suddenly form
the eyes I have desired,
which I bear sketched deep within my heart

New eyes. To be able to see the face of God in happenings, to be able to feel the hand of God in the events which happen, to be able to hear the voice of God in the circumstances of life - this is the dream which Saint John of the Cross helps us to acquire with this new outlook. A Christian can even feel the Beloved looking at him all the time.

But one might ask: How can I find *The eyes I have desired?* John's secret is simple: one must learn to live with Him. Familiarity with God is the trick. And to make this work easy, he even tells us where this God is:

Yes, indeed, o soul most favoured among all creatures, who so wishes to know the place where your Beloved is hidden, so that you can seek Him to unite yourself with Him, now I can tell you that you yourself are the place where He dwells and the inner room where He lies hidden. And this is some thing of great satisfaction to you to see that all your joy and your hope are so close, because they are in you, or, to express myself better, you cannot be without them.

What more do you want, o soul, and why seek more outside of you, when within you, you have your treasure, your joy, your satisfaction, your fulfillment, your kingdom, who is the Beloved of your soul, who your soul is searching for and longing for? Rejoice and be happy with him in your interior depths since you hold Him so close to yourself. Here want Him, here adore Him and do not go and seek Him outside of your self because you will distract your self and tire your self and you will not enjoy Him, for you will not find Him more surely and more close to you then when you seek Him within yourself.

Knowing this is terrific. Many times life becomes pitiless because we think that we are alone we face the problems of life alone. We think that we have to fend for ourselves. We believe that nobody understands us. We would like to talk to somebody and we find nobody who cares to listen. We want to share our lives with someone who can soothe us and apparently nobody has the time or the inclination for us.

Then it is reassuring to know that He is always there - so close as to be in ourselves, always ready to listen, to console, to cheer us up, to proffer good suggestions. No, we are never alone in our problems. And this God-in-us helps us to appreciate the God-in-others.

But even within us, God remains hidden! Even within us, God still plays hide and seek with us! He is not obvious! He is a hidden treasure.

But it is already a huge step in the right direction to know the place where He is hidden. We need to learn now how to seek Him. We need to learn to dig for this treasure.

Once, a nun asked Father John why whenever the frogs heard her coming towards them, they jumped at once into the monastery pond and hid in the very deepest water. With a smile on his lips, Father John explained that they did this because they were afraid of men, who might catch them. Hence they hide themselves in the water, where they feel safer. And the deeper they are in the water, the safer they feel. *Likewise, my daughter,* continued Father John, like the good spiritual director that he was, *you do the same: escape well from your enemies by launching yourself into the water that is God: hide yourself there because there you will be secure.*

This is what Saint John of the Cross believed. Since He is hidden within us, we too must conceal ourselves in order to find Him, since whoever wants to find something hidden, must hide himself and in secret enter the place where it is, and when he finds it, he will be hidden together with it.

Since your Beloved bridegroom is the treasure hidden in the field which is your soul, because of which the merchant sold all he had, it is wise that, in order to find him, after forgetting all you have and abandoning all creatures, you should hide in the same small interior room of your soul, and close the door behind you, that is, give up the wish for created things, and pray to your Father in secret, and you will love Him and taste Him and be happy with him in secret, I mean, in a way beyond what words and your senses can expect.

Perhaps this is what we have been missing in our lives. We have too much noise around us and within us. We arrive home and put our "walk man" on. The TV and the radio play all the time. At work machines make us dizzy with their noises. Cars are constantly screeching outside our windows. The sound of guns. Apparently we have lost the sense of silence ... Too much hustle-bustle. Our minds are too distracted. Always on the go, always breathless...

Saint John of the Cross is here proposing to us a way. A new way. More stillness within us. More silence around us. Time when we can be alone with Him.

Who knows what would happen if we start finding some time for ourselves and for God? He who loves, enjoys spending time with his beloved. The less people around, the better. Intimacy does not bear too many eyes watching it.

It is noteworthy, comments Saint John of the Cross, *that lovers have this quality; they enjoy each other's company alone, separated from all creatures, rather than in the company of others. The reason is that since love is a union of two people only, they want to speak only to each other.*

Let us rejoice, Beloved,
and let us go forth to behold
ourselves in your beauty
to the same mountain and to the hill,
to where the pure water flows,
and further, deep into the thicket.

So wrote the poet John of the Cross,

What is important is that we develop in ourselves this sense of the presence of God. We have to learn to remind ourselves that He is here.

When we were little, people often used to use God to frighten us. We used to visualize God as a policeman with a drawn baton, and each time we made a mistake we expected to get beaten about the head!

No. For Saint John of the Cross, God is someone who knows how to really love. In his writing, the word *beloved* in reference to Jesus Christ is used three hundred and thirty times and the word *redeemer* only twice.

It is not surprising that the Saint comes out with this wonderful piece of advice:

Take God as your bridegroom and your friend and walk with him all the time, and so you will not sin and you will learn to love, and things which you must do will go well.

God is a *bridegroom* and a *friend.* Somebody beautiful. Somebody who smiles at us and encourages us. How much more beautiful would our lives be if we remember that God is always with us because He is always within us.

The more we develop this art of the presence of God, the more meaningful our life becomes. We begin to be aware of the caresses which Jesus Christ showers on us throughout the day. We begin to realize that nothing happens by chance but everything is a deed of love on His part. Have you ever seen a lover denying anything to his bride? Do you believe that God would let anyone outdo Him in generosity even in the little things of every day?

Thus we begin to swim in the overflowing love of God, which starts becoming apparent in everything: in that telephone call, in that 'accidental' meeting with my friend, in that bus which took such a long time to arrive, in that letter which arrived just now, in that good news which they gave me... God knows how to fill His beloved with the kisses of His love.

And just where those who have not this continual contact with this good God, see misfortune, the Christian sees grace. Speaking of the Chapter of Madrid, which was the beginning of the campaign against him, John could say *here is the hand of God.* Others just saw the machinations of men. Nothing becomes a tragedy because this contact with the hidden God within us makes us positive persons.

John's companions recount to us how he loved to act out some scenes of the Gospel with the friars. Once, during recreation at Christmas time, he became so full of joy that he picked up baby Jesus and began to dance and sing with the Christ child in his arms: *Sweet and gentle Jesus, if your love can kill, this is the time!*

If only the love of Jesus not only filled us with joy but even killed us!

12 - When God falls in love

There is specialization in everything, medicine included. You find doctors specializing in eye problems, bone diseases, heart complaints, brain disorders, and so on. But it is strange that no one has ever specialized in curing long faces. If I were to open a clinic to cure long faces, I am sure that I would soon become very rich!!

It seems that everyone has become sick of this ailment. Some people complain about one thing, some about another. Some become bitter because their wives have become unbearable, others because their husbands have become more stressed and lose their temper more easily...

Some get better quickly and are soon smiling again; some spend hours, days and even months with an ugly, ugly face!

You find people who understand you and feel sorry for you and encourage you to keep going. There are others who pull you down, even passing stupid remarks which only irritate you more.

The problem is not outside us, but inside us ... that is how Saint John of the Cross reasoned.

From his youth he had to mix with many people of all kinds. He was very observant and human nature seemed to be an open book for him. Every person, he noted, has a very serious problem. This problem is the desires and hankerings of man, which never leave us in peace. They are always demanding, never satisfied. They are, he said, like spoilt brats, who want first one thing and then another. They are restless.

It is quite easy to agree with him. Our appetites never leave us alone. We always crave for more. One time it is money, next time is a better car, then a faster computer. Then our interior emotions - somebody telling us something and before we tell him what we think of his remark we are uneasy. Then we start getting worried about our health, or we notice we are getting fat and start planning how to start on a fat-free diet. Another time, the house seems too small and lacking all comforts and we begin to dream of another house, bigger and better. On another occasion it is the children because we cannot fathom them...

We have become a restless people - always jostling from one problem to another, from one worry to another. Nothing pleases us Everything bothers us. We are pleased with something and after a while we start planning what to do to acquire something else.

I do not know! There is nothing wrong with the things God provides us with - money, home, family, comfort, work, office-work... All is good. Therefore the problem must be in ourselves. We are like a cracked cup, comments Saint John of the Cross, no matter how much water we pour into it, the water keeps seeping out and gets lost. We are like a small bird which cannot fly no matter how hard it tries because it is tied down with a thread. And that thread keeps it tied down, a thin or a thick thread - it is irrelevant, notes the saint with much acumen.

A personal experience. After I had finished giving a series of talks, a young man approached me and said, *Father, the talk which struck me most was not the talk about the generation gap, or the one about problems in boy-girl relationships, or that about the environment at work or about drugs. No, the talk which affected me most deeply was when you talked to us about sadness and anguish, because, if you only know how miserable I feel sometimes. I feel like shouting and screaming! And when I try to tell this to my father, he is amazed and says, 'Why?, my son, what do you lack? don't you have all you need?!' As if,* continued this young man, *my father thinks he can remove my depression by filling up my stomach!!*

Sadness is a problem. Depression is problem which touches everyone. A plight which Saint John of the Cross also had to face.

A year after his escape from prison, we find Father John of the Cross superior of a place called El Calvario. A beautiful place full of greenery and valleys and mountains. Quite often he would take the friars out into the fields to pray there in the open instead of staying in the cramped conditions of the little chapel. The plants, the greenery, the mountain torrents, the trees, the expanse of the sky are very helpful to free our spirit and let it unfold up to God.

On Saturday evening, he used to enjoy going down to another village called Beas, to hear the confessions of and give talks to the Carmelite nuns who had a monastery there These nuns are cloistered nuns, namely they are women who never leave their monastery because for them God is enough.

Many times he would sleep there, spend the Sunday there, and return to his monastery on Monday. Always on foot, or occasionally on a donkey that someone may have lent him. While he was there, he used to keep himself busy - working in the garden, fixing tiles on the ground, helping out in the sacristy or in the church but most of his time was spent talking to the nuns.

In order to illustrate better his message, he once painted a drawing of a mountain which he called Mount Carmel. It is a very appealing design. There is the hill, which has a very high, dominant summit - it fills more than half the page. God lives on this summit - and here there is peace, security, beauty, wisdom. Everything is beautiful, everything is delightful. There are no laws. It is the place of God.

And not only of God. It is also the place of the man or woman who reaches the summit. God has one ambition in His mind: He wishes to seat man (that is you and I) at His own table and to feed us delightful and savory food. The thoughts of God are constantly focused on one thing: how can I fill man with all the possible goods that I have created for him!

When God falls in love with a soul, you cannot imagine how generous He can be. He starts showering the soul with gifts extravagantly. He starts giving out presents which no one else but He knows how to give. God is the greatest billionaire...

So, up on the peak is the abode of God. It is the place to which God can raise me up, if I let him! At the bottom of this hill, there are three roads. Two which meander and zigzag into nothing - they never make it to the the top. The other, a straight one, reaches the summit.

Which are the roads which lead to nowhere except to sadness and anguish? One is the road of money, honours, fancy ideas, diplomas, comfort... It is the road of those who strive hard to acquire more things, more respect, more esteem, a bigger car, a bigger house, a better education, more impressive certificates, more comforts... They strive and strive and find themselves with an empty heart, and often with empty hands! Saint John of the Cross jots down a little, tiny comment which is very provocative: *The more I desired to seek them the less I had them.* It is worth repeating it : *The more I desired to seek them the less I had them.*

This is our daily experience. We sweat to have a beautiful house and the moment we have it... we start fussing about mortgage, about termites, about the upkeep. We struggle hard to find a good suitable job and then we realize that this very work binds us down and does not let us enjoy even our children. What a pity! How foolish we can be!

The second road which leads nowhere is the road of consolation, security, pleasure... Yes, she serves the Lord, she certainly goes to Mass, she always says the rosary, brings up her children well, but God forbid, if the Lord does not abide by what she, such a good pious woman, desires, God forbid if an accident - her son dies, she crashes with her car, she goes to pray and feels no consolation - happens to her, such a devout godly woman, because then there is indeed havoc! *Why, is this how God treats me after serving Him so well! Everything always goes wrong for me, it would be better if I were like that call girl ... everything goes right for her!*

This is the road of those who serve the Lord so that they can suck back something from Him - health, consolation, happiness, rest, less trouble. Here also Saint John puts in a crisp short comment: *The more I hankered, the less I found.* God is not your servant. God is your leader!

Then there is the third road, the road in the middle. A straight road which leads you direct to God. On this road, he wrote only one word: NADA - nothing. Nothing repeated several times. It is the road of those who love nothing except God. They have learnt to put God first. Not money before God, but God before money. Not solace before God but God before solace. Not man before God, but God before man.

This does not mean that we must throw everything away. It means that we have to learn to use everything without becoming attached to anything. Things go wrong when I become attached to the statue instead of walking towards the Lord. Things go wrong when I become attached to a person instead of continuing walking towards the Lord.

Here Saint John of the Cross adds another concise short sentence *Now that I least desire them, I have them all without desire.* The Nothing leads to Everything.

Nothing is not something destructive or negative. We can use everything but we must learn not to become attached ... to anything. We can love everything but we cannot let our hearts pine for ... anything. And this out of love towards ourselves and towards the things that we are using. Out of love towards the persons we are relating with.

Many times what we call love is simple manipulation. Many times the objects of our affections destroy us.

Nobody can be put on a par with God! Nothing can be put on a par with God!

It is in this light that one must view the negation for which Saint John of the Cross became so famous. In his vision, detachment from everything is not the ascetic effort of a fanatic, but an intelligent awareness in the use of things. Use everything, love everything, appreciate everything, but hang on to nothing, be bound to nothing, because if you do, you will suffer and cause suffering in others. Build relationships with others but do not idolize anyone.

In this way you will experience the totality of God. Joy will increase. God will come down to you and fill you with Himself and so everything will acquire its appropriate focus in your life.

It is not surprising that Saint John of the Cross has been considered the Saint who comes closest to the atheist! The reason is obvious: he understood that God is greater than our minds and our hearts and therefore he destroys every image or idea which we could have of Him. God is not what we make Him. He is greater. He is more beautiful. He is different. John does not believe in the 'god' which many Christians believe in and who obscures the true God from the sight of others.

In Seville there was a group of eight novices, all young men full of energy and life. Their imagination was excited, full of the great and beautiful discoveries which the Spanish Conquistadores were making in the New World. Their superior was worried because he felt they were too distracted, their minds were too muddled! He thought it would be better to dismiss them all as he considered them unsuitable for the Discalced Carmelite way of life. Father John of the Cross, the Vicar provincial at the time, went to see, to understand what was going on. He quickly realized... The crazy ones were not the young friars! The crazy one was the master of novices, who was taxing them with six hours of prayer a day! *Don't you see?!*, he remarked, *Less hours of prayer, more free time and more work in the garden .... and you will see how things will improve!*

This is what God does. When you climb the hill of Mount Carmel, you become familiar with God, and because you become familiar with God, you will understand men better...

13 - Climb onto the Cross... and rest

Darkness exists in life. There are times when you understand nothing. You look upwards and see nothing but clouds. You feel a lot of pain and you ask yourself in your heart:

But why? Where is God in all this? How can He just sit quietly and nonchalant ly up there in the heavens?! Why does he not do something?

War, the killing of so many innocent victims because of the folly of a single man. Illness. The agony of famine. Rampant injustice.

You find yourself alone - forgotten by those for whom you care. You lose the meaning in life... and you find yourself alienating yourself in drinking, watching television till two in the morning, hard work, going out... God is so far away.

A seven year old boy killed in a stupid, pointless traffic accident. A cousin dies eaten up by cancer and leaves three children orphans. A son is born deformed. *God has abandoned me... He does not hear me..."* An accusation? A plea for help?

Saint John of the Cross gives a name to these experiences. He calls them DARK NIGHTS. The passive night.

He knows what suffering is because he experienced it. He knows what he is talking about.

Today the problem of pain has become more acute, because we live in a society which is terrified of suffering.

A headache? Take a panadol. Warm? Put on the fan. Cold? Switch on the heater. This is lessening our level of resistance. We are becoming too soft. And therefore, the moment pain appears in our life, we panic dreadfully.

What is the message of Saint John for those who are experiencing their dark night?

It is an important message because it is a message of faith. He learnt one thing, a simple, basic truth. A gem. In the darkness God transforms you.

It is not true that suffering is a senseless chastisement from God *He deserved it! He asked for it. God always pays you back!* So many sins, so much punishment in return! No!
God penalizes no one. He understands us too well. He has infinite mercy. He knows that we are weak and that we fall all the time.

Neither is it true that suffering comes to us so that God can test us. Test us on what?! He knows us well enough and knows how easily anger and despair are activated in us when we are confronted with pain.

Nor does suffering come to us so that we may resign ourselves. Resign ourselves. *Well, what can you do? Patience. Since this is what God wills, it is surely for your good, my son...* Wrong again! Nobody takes an attitude of passive resignation before a free gift!

This is the whole point. The cross is a gift!

This is the deep meaning of the dark night. In the first part of his book **The Ascent of Mount Carmel**, John writes these words: *The darkness and suffering, both spiritual and material which* fortunate *souls usually suffer in their journey to this high state of perfection are so numerous and so deep that we cannot fully understand them*.

He calls the person who is passing through darkness and suffering *fortunate*.

Fortunate because suffering shows me who I am - I am not a 'god' even if I may wish to be so. It puts me in my place. It puts me in my real dimension. It educates me. There is a lot of divine pedagogy in the dark night.

Suffering becomes precious because it teaches me to rest on what is solid. I who built my life on the sand of money, family, success, a clean house... through the cross can learn to rest on God - the rock which does not move, the deliverer who redeems... Pursuit of career is empty, my money will run out, my strength will fade away, friends may leave me, my husband will die... ONLY GOD REMAINS.

Suffering thus becomes a treasure because it teaches me to turn my eyes towards Him. It teaches me to cry to Him for help. It teaches me to seize Him. It was in his cross that Abraham discovered that God provides. It was when he was drowning that Peter found out that Jesus saves. In your suffering, you will discover that God cares very deeply about you. *He knows very well and very surely how to bring forth good from evil.*

It is not true that, before your suffering and my suffering, God sat back on his throne commiserating with us from heaven. He made definite steps towards us. He became man. He suffered under Pontius Pilate, was crucified, died and was buried. He suffered with us and for us. After this revelation of his Son, God *remained as if dumb, because He had nothing more to say.* He showed us how much He loved us by sharing our suffering. So that we will not suffer... if we learn to live our suffering with Him.

Jesus Christ did not come to remove suffering and difficulties. He did not come to do what you ought to do yourself. But his cross means that HE IS NEVER FAR FROM YOU AND HE WILL GIVE YOU THE STRENGTH TO FACE LIFE IN SUCH A WAY THAT IT WILL NOT DESTROY YOU BUT BUILD YOU UP TO REAL LIFE, ETERNAL LIFE.

It is suffering which can bring you face to face with Jesus Christ today. *Climb on to the cross and find your rest,* Isaac of Gaza used to say. And Saint John of the Cross always linked the cross with repose.

When he changed his name from John *of Saint Mattias* to John *of the Cross* he did this for a good reason. He was not a crazy sadist who loved suffering. He simply realized that in the cross, one finds rest. There is a mystery - the mystery of Easter, the passage from death to life.

He had certainly read the classic of Carmelite spirituality of that time: "The Institutions of the First Monks", which speaks clearly of this: *as one who is tied to this tree of the cross does not think of the present, forgets the past and pays no attention to the future, and so the yearnings of the body do not move and he can keep his heart fixed on where he is going, so the monk should keep himself bound to the love of God and keep the eyes of his soul always fixed there where he always wishes to go.*

He suffers but he is calm. He suffers but he knows that this pain is stripping him from his stupid pride and making him small. And so, he begins to look around him and, maybe for the first time, he begins to appreciate and to feel compassion.

This is what John of the Cross believes. This is what you can believe.

Yes, Christianity is good news because it sheds light even on the pain which, more or less, always accompanies us during our life. Christianity helps us to react to pain in a positive way.

Indeed no one can understand pain, but everybody feels it, especially when it affects yourself or someone you love. Everybody tries to avoid it. And this is right. When Saint John of the Cross had an opportunity to escape from prison, he escaped!

But sometimes pain comes upon us and we cannot avoid it - an illness, a boy knocked down by a car, the death of someone you love, the breakdown of your marriage, an injustice at work, a calumny against you...

The Lord wants to give us the grace to understand one thing: suffering, if we know how to tackle it, can mature us. If we are able to accept pain, it can make us grow. But, if we rebel against it, we will be simply creating more tension within us and we shall suffer more, even physically. Therefore, when you cannot escape pain, enter into it. *Pick up your cross* the Master used to say. And thus you will be making a great step forward.

Thus pain does not remain an enemy, something dreadful against which you must fight constantly but it becomes a friend, even a part of your life. God is not wicked. He does not send you pain to crush you, He permits it in your life to ripen you.

If you accept pain unwillingly, then it will wear you out. But if you accept pain willingly, then it will beautify you.

The words of the Saint are clear.

The purest suffering produces the purest understanding.
He who seeks not the cross of Christ seeks not the glory of Christ.
Crucified inwardly and outwardly with Christ, you will live in this life in fullness and in deep satisfaction of

the soul, and so you will possess your soul in patience.

If only we could understand that we cannot reach the depths of the wood of God's wisdom and riches except by entering the depths of the wood of many sorts of suffering ˘ To enter this fullness of wisdom, the door is the cross, which is narrow and few are those who wish to enter it although many are those who wish for the joy one can find by doing so.

When your mind stops on something, you will be stopping in your journey towards the All, because, so that you can pass through all things in your journey towards the All, you must deny yourself in all things and for all things. And when you come to have the All, it is important that you wish for nothing in Him, for if you seek something in possessing everything you will not be placing your treasure with total purity in God.

I have fought the good fight." This is how Saint Paul ends his second letter to Timothy. Christian life is a struggle and the greatest fighter was Christ. The marvelous thing is that He is going to fight this struggle in me and with me. This is what Moses says to the Israelites: *You will never again see the Egyptians who you see before you today. This Lord will fight for you without you yourselves doing anything.* (Exodus 14,14s)

How foolish we are to want to put aside that which can solve all the problems of our life, namely, the cross...

14 - Close Friends

I know a lady to whom the Lord chose to give some of these great graces - or rather I know two (one is a man). These two were always very anxious in their hearts to serve the Lord at their own expense, without having these outstanding graces; and they used to so long for suffering that they used to complain to the Lord about the graces which He lavished on them, to the extent that if they could, they would have avoided receiving them, to see what they would have done without them.

Here is Teresa of Jesus speaking of herself and *of a man* -   Saint John of the Cross. Both had an impressive love for Jesus Christ. Both suffered exceedingly for Jesus Christ. That is the reason why they were both happy. The Lord brought them together to start a new style of religious life in the Church - the Discalced Carmelite family.

Above all, to initiate a strong movement of interiority in the Church.

These two saints, Teresa and John, lived at about the same time - Spain of the sixteenth century. She was born in 1515, he in 1542 - twenty seven years difference.   He found himself an orphan at the age of eight, she lost her mother at the age of twelve. He was to experience hunger and misery at home. She lived a life of riches with many comforts.

At the age of twenty one, both entered Carmel. One escaped from home because her father was not happy with her decision. The other preferred Carmel even though he had good chances of acquiring good career positions with other orders. They both felt that the Lord was calling them to live the Gospel without any frills - everything or nothing.

One dreamed and strived to create a style of religious life built on prayer and joy in the confines of the cloister, the other wished to join the Carthusians, because these live a more austere and recollected life.

Totally different characters. She was the joyful type, who enjoyed companionship, always on the go, savoured a laugh herself and knew how to make other people laugh. Nuncio Sega even called her a *vagrant woman*. He was the quiet type, who loved solitude, never spoke about himself, he loved nature, an artist, a poet, loving everything that is beautiful

It was September/October1567 when Mother Teresa of Jesus met for the first time Father John of the Cross. She was 52 years old, a mature woman, already plunged firmly and delightfully in the way of intimacy with the Lord. She had already opened the first convent of enclosed Carmelite nuns at San Josè, Avila. Now she was at Medina del Campo to found her second house. She was feeling ever more strongly the need that Jesus should have more firm friends who would fight the good fight against the enemies of the kingdom, using the powerful weapon of prayer.

He had just been ordained. He had not even finished his studies in Salamanca. He was at Medina del Campo to say his first Solemn High Mass. Present were his mother and his brother Francisco with his wife. He is only 25 years old and is passing through a deep interior crisis. Although the Carmelite monastery of San Andrew where he lived, was a good monastery, all the same he felt dissatisfied.

Teresa, being the very practical woman she was, persuaded him to join her and take part in the adventure of beginning the Carmelite reform for the friars. Teresa was very impressed with him: *when I spoke to him, I was genuinely pleased with him.* He accepted, on condition that the plans should not take too long. One can see here his true character - anxious and full of zeal where the business of his Lord is involved. A lover is always impatient!

Despite their great differences in character and age, they both concur closely in their vision. Both were not afraid to take risks. They risked in their spiritual lives. They risked in their plans. The Christian is willing to follow in the footsteps of his Master ... He even risked his life for us.

Teresa taught John the style of the new life in Carmel - a balance between prayer, joy and penance. She took him with her to Vallidolid when she went to open her third monastery there. In her letters she calls him *a man of heaven, divine, my little Seneca.* It was she who found a hamlet at Duruelo and gave him some images of Christ and the new habit of the Discalced Carmelite friars so that he could begin the life of the Carmelite Reform.

In 1571 Mother Teresa asked her superiors to allow Father John of the Cross to become spiritual director of the nuns of the Incarnation - an enormous monastery of more than 150 nuns, lots of mediocrity and abundant compromises. Using a great deal of compassion and gentleness he was able to create a healthy environment of sisterly love. Now, at the age of 30, he is the director of Mother Teresa. He helps her greatly. He understands her and encourages her in her mystical experiences. She calls him *the father of my soul.*

At the age of thirty-five his own companions arrest him and put him in prison for more than eight months. He who follows the master is not surprised if he finishes hanging up on a cross like Him. Teresa was extremely preoccupied because she feared he might die there.

When he escapes from Toledo, he finds himself in Andalucia, far from *Mother.* She too feels his absence : *you cannot understand the loneliness I feel because of his absence. After he had gone, I could find no one else like him in the whole of Castille who encourages others with so much fire in their way towards heaven.*

They met for the last time on 28th November 1581. After her death, he worked very hard so that the friars should publish her writings. *Few are the souls who go so far,* he comments about her.

Teresa loved him because in him she saw a spiritual, affable and wise friar. John loved her because he saw in her a woman who lived with zest the adventure of intimacy with God up to the very end. She did not stop half way. He was very grateful to her.

Both wrote down their experiences. Beautiful writings full of life and above all, full of genuine experiences. Teresa writes as if she was talking. John writes in a more studious and elaborate fashion. But in the writings of both there is life, there is love, there is God.

Both use many exquisite images - an interior castle, the night, the flame, the mountain, a silkworm becoming a butterfly, a garden, the sun shining on a window pane ...

Both understood one thing. They understood that in life the heart is all important. Find someone who loves you fully and you will enjoy bliss.

The only One who can love you fully is God.

Hence life is beautiful if you learn to live it with God. *God alone suffices,* Teresa would say. *One who does not acknowledge God in his life, recognizes nothing,* John used to say.

In both of them there was this love towards God. Necessarily there was born in them a desire for union. On one hand God, who wants to raise man up to himself, and wants to make out of man God. On the other hand, man, amazed and forcefully drawn to this Love.

Teresa and John believed in this vision. So they kept going ahead without wavering, convinced that God would keep His word. *With determination,* Teresa would add. *With a lot gentleness,* John would comment. *O most sweet love of God, so little known, he who found its source, has found life!*

If the love of one man for another was so strong that it was able to bind one soul to another, what shall we say of the bond which binds the soul to God the bridegroom, fruit of the love of the soul for God?! Even more so, since God himself is the principal Lover, He who in the omnipotence of His profound love absorbs the soul with greater rapidity and strength than that with which a river absorbs a wind borne drop of morning dew...

Hence we see God doing all that he can to see that this project of love succeeds. He works, strives, places us in favourable situations, sends us events which draw us to Him, destroys all our idols, dispatches angels...

The more man discovers this love the more he is amazed. Amazed to discover how God, God himself, can possibly love him as he is, full of sins and nonsense. He is simply overcome when he sees how God has toiled and is now striving to marry him or her - a simple normal man or woman.

Thus spontaneously there arises in him the wish to do all he can becomes a game of love between man and God.

On the side of man, a whole process of purification starts. Saint John of the Cross calls it a night. It is a labour done by God and by man. The one who works hardest is God. The passive night is more powerful than the active night. He detaches himself from everything because *what difference is it if a bird is tied down by a thread or by a thick string? No matter how thin the thread, the bird who is tied down cannot fly unless the binding is broken; in the same way, the soul which is still attached to something, no matter how much virtue it possesses, cannot achieve the freedom of divine union.*

God becomes a fire which burns the dry wood of the soul of man until at last the soul becomes a splendid living red flame... The soul is now in the seventh mansion and there it encounters the light which is God the Father, God the Son and God the Holy Spirit. Man becomes God...

Once Mother Teresa and Father John were speaking together in the parlour of the monastery of Encarnacion of Avila. The Sister in charge of the door was surprised to find them both in ecstasy! *What happened, Mother?* the nuns asked later. She smiled her typical smile and answered: *What can you expect!? One cannot speak to Father John about this God so full of beauty, without going into ecstasy!!*

This was their vision. This could be your vision too. Not a lot of devotions and ceremonials but a strong friendship with Him. Teresa and John sat down at the table of the Lord and they came out full of enthusiasm. Shall we also have this opportunity?

How many fantastic things are ready for those who love...

A final reflection. I wonder why when God wishes to do great things, He always brings together a man and woman?!

Courage! The adventure is still ahead!

□

CHRIST CRUCIFIED
A DRAWING BY ST. JOHN OF THE CROSS

His Writings

Avila, Beas, Granada
Cloistered nuns
Carmelites.
Father John of the Cross loved them immensely
and so he wished to help them meet and love God
ever more and more.

After a talk or after spiritual direction
to help them on their journey,
he would often write short sentences
which he would give to them.
An aid for meditation.
An aid for reflection.
Billettes ... that's what they called them.

He himself gathered some of them and
gave them the beautiful name of
'Dichos de luz y amor' - 'Sayings of light and love'.

They are short sentences,
the fruit of his experience of God and man.
They are full of life, doctrine and artistic sensitivity.

They are like arrows penetrating the heart.
Let them wound you.
And fill you with joy.

Prologue

O my God and my delight, for your love I have also desired to give my soul to composing these sayings of light and love concerning you. Since, although I can express them in words, I do not have the works and virtues they imply (which is what pleases you, O my Lord, more than the words and wisdom they contain), may others, perhaps stirred by them, go forward in your service and love You - in which I am wanting. I will thereby find consolation, that these sayings be an occasion for your finding in others the things that I lack.

Lord, you love discretion, you love light, you love love; these three you love above the other operations of the soul. Hence these will be sayings of discretion for the wayfarer, light for the way, and of love in the wayfaring. May there be nothing of worldly rhetoric in them or the long winded and dry eloquence of weak and artificial human wisdom, which never pleases you. Let us speak to the heart with words bathed in sweetness and love that do indeed please you, removing obstacles and stumbling blocks from the paths of many souls who unknowingly trip and unconsciously walk in the path of error - poor souls who think they are right in what concerns the following of your beloved Son, our Lord Jesus Christ, in becoming like him, imitating his life, actions, and virtues, and the form of his nakedness and purity of spirit.

Father of mercies, come to our aid, for without you, Lord, we can do nothing.

1. The Lord has always revealed to mortals the treasures of his wisdom and his spirit, but now that the face of evil bares itself more and more, so does the Lord bare his treasures more.

2. O Lord, my God, who will seek you with simple and pure love, and not find that you are all one can desire, for you show yourself first and go out to meet those who seek you?

3. Though the path is plain and smooth for people of good will, those who walk it will not travel far, and will do so only with difficulty if they do not have good feet, courage, and tenacity of spirit.

4. It is better to be burdened and in company with the strong, than to be unburdened and with the weak. When you are burdened you are close to God, your strength, who abides with the afflicted. When you are relieved of the burden you are close to yourself, your own weakness; for virtue and strength of soul grow and are confirmed in the trials of patience.

5. Whoever wants to stand alone without the support of a master and guide will be like the tree that stands alone in a field without a proprietor. No matter how much the tree bears, passersby will pick the fruit before it ripens.

6. A tree that is cultivated and guarded through the care of its owner produces its fruit at the expected time.

7. The virtuous soul that is alone and without a master

is like a lone burning coal; it will grow colder rather than hotter.

8. Those who fall alone remain alone in their fall, and they value their soul little since they entrust it to themselves alone.

9. If you do not fear falling alone, do you presume that you will rise up alone? Consider how much more can be accomplished by two together than by one alone.

10. Whoever falls while heavily laden will find it difficult to rise under the burden.

11. The blind person who falls will not be able to get up alone; the blind person who does get up alone will go off on the wrong road.

12. God desires the smallest degree of purity of conscience in you more than all the works you can perform.

13. God desires the least degree of obedience and submissiveness more than all those services you think of rendering him.

14. God values in you the inclination to dryness and suffering for love of him more than all the consolations, spiritual visions, and meditations you could possibly have.

15. Deny your desires and you will find what your heart longs for. For how do you know if any desire of yours is according to God?

16. O sweetest love of God, so little known, whoever has found this rich mine is at rest!

17. Since a double measure of bitterness must follow the doing of your own will, do not do it even though you remain in single bitterness.

18. The soul that carries within itself the least appetite for worldly things bears more unseemliness and impurity in its journey to God than if it were troubled by all the hideous and annoying temptations and darknesses describable; for, so long as it does not consent to these temptations, a soul thus tried can approach God confidently, by doing the will of His Majesty, who proclaims: Come to me, all you who labour and are heavily burdened, and I will refresh you [Mt. 11:28].

19. The soul that in aridity and trial submits to the dictates of reason is more pleasing to God than one that does everything with consolation, yet fails in this submission.

20. God is more pleased by one work, however small, done secretly, without desire that it be known, than a thousand done with the desire that people know of them. Those who work for God with purest love not only care nothing about whether others see their works, but do not even seek that God himself knows of them. Such persons would not cease to render God the same services, with the same joy and purity of love, even if God were never to know of these.

21. The pure and whole work done for God in a pure heart merits a whole kingdom for its owner.

22. A bird caught in bird-lime has a twofold task: It must free itself and cleanse itself. And by satisfying their appetites, people suffer in a twofold way: They must detach themselves and, after being detached, clean themselves of what has clung to them.

23. Those who do not allow their appetites to carry them away will soar in their spirit as swiftly as the bird that lacks no feathers.

24. The fly that clings to honey hinders its flight, and the soul that allows itself attachment to spiritual sweetness hinders its own liberty and contemplation.

25. Withdraw from creatures if you desire to preserve, clear and simple in your soul, the image of God. Empty your spirit and withdraw far from them and you will walk in divine light, for God is not like creatures.

26. The very pure spirit does not bother about the regard of others or human respect, but communes inwardly with God, alone and in solitude as to all forms, and with delightful tranquility, for the knowledge of God is received in divine silence.

27. A soul enkindled with love is a gentle, meek, humble, and patient soul.

28. A soul that is hard because of self love grows harder. O good Jesus, if you do not soften it, it will ever

continue in its natural hardness.

29. If you lose an opportunity you will be like one who lets the bird fly away; you will never get it back.

30. I didn't know you, my Lord, because I still desired to know and relish things.

31. Well and good if all things change, Lord God, provided we are rooted in you.

32. One thought alone is worth more than the entire world, hence God alone is worthy of it.

33. For the insensible, what you do not feel; for the sensible, the senses; and for the spirit of God, thought.

34. Reflect that your guardian angel does not always move your desire for an action, but he does always enlighten your reason. Hence, in order to practice virtue do not wait until you feel like it, for your reason and intellect are sufficient.

35. When fixed on something else, one's appetite leaves no room for the angel to move it.

36. My spirit has become dry because it forgets to feed on you.

37. What you most seek and desire you will not find by this way of yours, nor through high contemplation, but in much humility and submission of heart.

38. Do not tire yourself, for you will not enter into the savour and sweetness of spirit if you do not apply yourself to the mortification of all this that you desire.

39. Reflect that the most delicate flower loses its fragrance and withers fastest; therefore guard yourself against seeking to walk in a spirit of delight, for you will not be constant. Choose rather for yourself a robust spirit, detached from everything, and you will discover abundant peace and sweetness, for delicious and durable fruit is gathered in a cold and dry climate.

40. Bear in mind that your flesh is weak and that no worldly thing can comfort or strengthen your spirit, for what is born of the world is world and what is born of the flesh is flesh. The good spirit is born only of the Spirit of God, who communicates himself neither through the world nor through the flesh.

41. Be attentive to your reason in order to do what it tells you concerning the way to God. It will be more valuable before your God than all the works you perform without this attentiveness and all the spiritual delights you seek.

42. Blessed are they who, setting aside their own pleasure and inclination, consider things according to reason and justice before doing them.

43. If you make use of your reason, you are like one who eats substantial food; but if you are moved by the satisfaction of your will, you are like one who eats insipid fruit.

44. Lord, you return gladly and lovingly to lift up the one who offends you, but I do not turn to raise and honour the one who annoys me.

45. O mighty Lord, if a spark from the empire of your justice effects so much in the mortal ruler who governs the nations, what will your all-powerful justice do with the righteous and the sinner?

46. If you purify your soul of attachments and desires, you will understand things spiritually. If you deny your appetite for them, you will enjoy their truth, understanding what is certain in them.

47. O Lord, my God, you are no stranger to those who do not estrange themselves from you. How do they say that it is you who absent yourself?

48. That person has truly mastered all things who is not moved to joy by the satisfaction they afford or saddened by their insipidness.

49. If you wish to attain holy recollection, you will do so not by receiving but by denying.

50. Going everywhere, my God, with you, everywhere things will happen as I desire for you.

51. Souls will be unable to reach perfection who do not strive to be content with having nothing, in such fashion that their natural and spiritual desire is satisfied with emptiness; for this is necessary in order to reach the highest

tranquility and peace of spirit. Hence the love of God in the pure and simple soul is almost continually in act.

52. Since God is inaccessible, be careful not to concern yourself with all that your faculties can comprehend and your senses feel, so that you do not become satisfied with less and thus lose the lightness of soul needed for going to him.

53. The soul that journeys to God, but does not shake off its cares and quiet its appetites, is like one who drags a cart uphill.

54. It is not God's will that a soul be disturbed by anything or suffer trials, for if one suffers trials in the adversities of the world it is because of a weakness in virtue. The perfect soul rejoices in what afflicts the imperfect one.

55. This way of life contains very little business and bustling, and demands mortification of the will more than knowledge. The less one takes of things and pleasures the farther one advances along this way.

56. Think not that pleasing God lies so much in doing a great deal as in doing it with good will, without possessiveness and human respect.

57. When evening comes, you will be examined in love.[21] Learn to love as God desires to be loved and abandon your own ways of acting.

58. See that you do not interfere in the affairs of

others, nor even allow them to pass through your memory; for perhaps you will be unable to accomplish your own task.

59.   Because the virtues you have in mind do not shine in your neighbour, do not think that your neighbour will not be precious in God's sight for reasons that you have not in mind.

60.   Human beings know neither how to rejoice properly nor how to grieve properly, for they do not understand the distance between good and evil.

61.   See that you are not suddenly saddened by the adversities of this world, for you do not know the good they bring, being ordained in the judgments of God for the everlasting joy of the elect.

62.   Do not rejoice in temporal prosperity, since you do not know if it gives you assurance of eternal life.

63.   In tribulation, immediately draw near to God with trust, and you will receive strength, enlightenment, and instruction.

64.   In joys and pleasures, immediately draw near to God in fear and truth, and you will be neither deceived nor involved in vanity.

65.   Take God for your bridegroom and friend, and walk with him continually; and you will not sin and will learn to love, and the things you must do will work out prosperously for you.

66. You will without labour subject the nations and bring things to serve you if you forget them and yourself as well.

67. Abide in peace, banish cares, take no account of all that happens, and you will serve God according to his good pleasure, and rest in him.

68. Consider that God reigns only in the peaceful and disinterested soul.

69. Although you perform many works, if you do not deny your will and submit yourself, losing all solicitude about yourself and your affairs, you will not make progress.

70. What does it profit you to give God one thing if he asks of you another? Consider what it is God wants, and then do it. You will as a result satisfy your heart better than with something toward which you yourself are inclined.

71. How is it you dare to relax so fearlessly, since you must appear before God to render an account of the least word and thought?

72. Reflect that many are called but few are chosen [Mt. 22:14] and that, if you are not careful, your perdition is more certain than your salvation, especially since the path to eternal life is so constricted [Mt. 7:14].

73. Do not rejoice vainly, for you know how many sins you have committed and you do not know how you stand before God; but have fear together with confidence.

74. Since, when the hour of reckoning comes, you will be sorry for not having used this time in the service of God, why do you not arrange and use it now as you would wish to have done were you dying?

75. If you desire that devotion be born in your spirit and that the love of God and the desire for divine things increase, cleanse your soul of every desire, attachment, and ambition in such a way that you have no concern about anything. Just as a sick person is immediately aware of good health once the bad humour has been thrown off and a desire to eat is felt, so will you recover your health, in God, if you cure yourself as was said. Without doing this, you will not advance no matter how much you do.

76. If you desire to discover peace and consolation for your soul and to serve God truly, do not find your satisfaction in what you have left behind, because in that which now concerns you may be as impeded as you were before, or even more. But leave as well all these other things and attend to one thing alone that brings all these with it (namely, holy solitude, together with prayer and spiritual and divine reading), and persevere there in forgetfulness of all things.

For if these things are not incumbent on you, you will be more pleasing to God in knowing how to guard and perfect yourself than by gaining all other things together; what profit would there be for one to gain the whole world and suffer the loss of one's soul? [Mt. 16:26].

Prayer of a Soul Taken with Love [19]

Lord God, my Beloved, if you still remember my sins in such a way that you do not do what I beg of you, do your will concerning them, my God, which is what I most desire, and exercise your goodness and mercy, and you will be known through them.

And if you are waiting for my good works so as to hear my prayer through their means, grant them to me, and work them for me, and the sufferings you desire to accept, and let it be done.

But if you are not waiting for my works, what is it that makes you wait, my most clement Lord? Why do you delay?

For if, after all, I am to receive the grace and mercy that I entreat of you in your Son, take my mite [20] , since you desire it, and grant me this blessing, since you also desire that.

Who can free themselves from lowly manners and limitations if you do not lift them to yourself, my God, in purity of love? How will human beings begotten and nurtured in lowliness rise up to you, Lord, if you do not raise them with your hand that made them?

You will not take from me, my God, what you once gave me in your only Son, Jesus Christ, in whom you gave me all I desire. Hence I rejoice that if I wait for you, you will not delay.

With what procrastinations do you wait, since from this very moment you can love God in your heart?

Mine are the heavens and mine is the earth. Mine are the nations, the just are mine, and mine the sinners. The angels are mine, and the Mother of God, and all things are mine; and God himself is mine and for me, because Christ is mine and all for me. What do you ask, then, and seek, my soul? Yours is all of this, and all is for you.

Do not engage yourself in something less or pay heed to the crumbs that fall from your Father's table. Go forth and exult in your Glory! Hide yourself in it and rejoice, and you will obtain the supplications of your heart.[3]

MAXIMS ON LOVE [22]

1. Bridle your tongue and your thoughts very much, direct your affection habitually toward God, and your spirit will be divinely enkindled.

2. Feed not your spirit on anything but God. Cast off concern about things, and bear peace and recollection in your heart.

3. Keep spiritually tranquil in a loving attentiveness to God,[23] and when it is necessary to speak, let it be with the same calm and peace.

4. Preserve a habitual remembrance of eternal life, recalling that those who hold themselves the lowest and poorest and least of all will enjoy the highest dominion and glory in God.

5. Rejoice habitually in God, who is your salvation [Lk. 1:47], and reflect that it is good to suffer in any way for him who is good.

6. Reflect how necessary it is to be enemies of self and to walk to perfection by the path of holy rigor, and understand that every word spoken without the order of obedience is laid to your account by God.

7. Have an intimate desire that His Majesty grant you what he knows you lack for his honour.

8. Crucified inwardly and outwardly with Christ, you will live in this life with fullness and satisfaction of soul, and possess your soul in patience [Lk. 21:19].

9. Preserve a loving attentiveness to God with no desire to feel or understand any particular thing concerning him.

10. Keep habitual confidence in God, esteeming in yourself and in your Sisters those things that God most values, which are spiritual goods.

11. Enter within yourself and work in the presence of your Bridegroom, who is ever present loving you.

12. Be hostile to admitting into your soul things that of themselves have no spiritual substance, lest they make you lose your liking for devotion and recollection.

13. Let Christ crucified be enough for you, and with him suffer and take your rest, and hence annihilate yourself in all inward and outward things.

14. Endeavour always that things be not for you, nor you for them, but forgetful of all, abide in recollection with

your Bridegroom.

15. Have great love for trials and think of them as but a small way of pleasing your Bridegroom, who did not hesitate to die for you.

16. Bear fortitude in your heart against all things that move you to that which is not God, and be a friend of the Passion of Christ.

17. Be interiorly detached from all things and do not seek pleasure in any temporal thing, and your soul will concentrate on goods you do not know.

18. The soul that walks in love neither tires others nor grows tired.

19. The poor one who is naked will be clothed; and the soul that is naked of desires and whims, God will clothe with his purity, pleasure, and will.

20. There are souls that wallow in the mire like animals, and there are others that soar like birds, which purify and cleanse themselves in the air.

21. The Father spoke one Word, which was his Son, and this Word he speaks always in eternal silence, and in silence must it be heard by the soul.

22. We must adjust our trials to ourselves, and not ourselves to our trials.

23. He who seeks not the cross of Christ seeks not the glory of Christ.

24. To be taken with love for a soul, God does not look on its greatness, but on the greatness of its humility.

25. Whoever is ashamed to confess me before others, I shall be ashamed to confess before My Father, says the Lord [Mt. 10:33].

26. Frequent combing gives the hair more luster and makes it easier to comb; a soul that frequently examines its thoughts, words, and deeds, which are its hair, doing all things for the love of God, will have lustrous hair. Then the Bridegroom will look on the neck of the bride and thereby be captivated; and will be wounded by one of her eyes, that is, by the purity of intention she has in all she does. If in combing hair one wants it to have luster, one begins from the crown. All our works must begin from the crown (the love of God) if we wish them to be pure and lustrous.

27. Heaven is stable and is not subject to generation; and souls of a heavenly nature are stable and not subject to the engendering of desires or of anything else, for in their way they resemble God who does not move forever.

28. Eat not in forbidden pastures (those of this life), because blessed are they who hunger and thirst for justice, for they will be satisfied [Mt. 5:6]. What God seeks, he being himself God by nature, is to make us gods through participation, just as fire converts all things into fire.

29. All the goodness we possess is lent to us, and God considers it his own work. God and his work is God.

30. Wisdom enters through love, silence, and mortification. It is great wisdom to know how to be silent and to look at neither the remarks, nor the deeds, nor the lives of others.

31. All for me and nothing for you.

32. All for you and nothing for me.

33. Allow yourself to be taught, allow yourself to receive orders, allow yourself to be subjected and despised, and you will be perfect.

34. Any appetite causes five kinds of harm in the soul: first, disquiet; second, turbidity; third, defilement; fourth, weakness; fifth, obscurity.[24]

35. Perfection does not lie in the virtues that the soul knows it has, but in the virtues that our Lord sees in it. This is a closed book; hence one has no reason for presumption, but must remain prostrate on the ground with respect to self.

36. Love consists not in feeling great things but in having great detachment and in suffering for the Beloved.

37. The entire world is not worthy of a human being's thought, for this belongs to God alone; any thought,

therefore, not centered on God is stolen from him.

38. Not all the faculties and senses have to be employed in things, but only those that are required; as for the others, leave them unoccupied for God.

39. Ignoring the imperfections of others, preserving silence and a continual communion with God will eradicate great imperfections from the soul and make it the possessor of great virtues.

40. There are three signs of inner recollection: first, a lack of satisfaction in passing things; second, a liking for solitude and silence, and an attentiveness to all that is more perfect; third, the considerations, meditations and acts that formerly helped the soul now hinder it, and it brings to prayer no other support than faith, hope, and love.

41. If a soul has more patience in suffering and more forbearance in going without satisfaction, the sign is that it is being more proficient in virtue.

42. The traits of the solitary bird are five: first, it seeks the highest place; second, it withstands no company; third, it holds its beak in the air; fourth, it has no definite colour; fifth, it sings sweetly. These traits must be possessed by the contemplative soul. It must rise above passing things, paying no more heed to them than if they did not exist. It must likewise be so fond of silence and solitude that it does not tolerate the company of another creature. It must hold its beak in the air of the Holy Spirit, responding to his inspirations, that by so doing it may become worthy of his

company. It must have no definite colour, desiring to do nothing definite other than the will of God. It must sing sweetly in the contemplation and love of its Bridegroom.[25]

43. Habitual voluntary imperfections that are never completely overcome not only hinder the divine union, but also the attainment of perfection. Such imperfections are: the habit of being very talkative; a small unconquered attachment, such as to a person, to clothing, to a cell, a book, or to the way food is prepared, and to other conversations and little satisfactions in tasting things, in knowing, and hearing, and the like.

44. If you wish to glory in yourself, but do not wish to appear ignorant and foolish, discard the things that are not yours and you will have glory in what remains. But certainly if you discard all that is not yours, nothing will be left, since you must not glory in anything if you do not want to fall into vanity. But let us descend now especially to those graces, the gifts that make people pleasing in God's sight. It is certain that you must not glory in these gifts, for you do not even know if you possess them.

45. Oh, how sweet your presence will be to me, you who are the supreme good! I must draw near you in silence and uncover your feet that you may be pleased to unite me to you in marriage [Ruth 3:7], and I will not rest until I rejoice in your arms. Now I ask you, Lord, not to abandon me at any time in my recollection, for I am a squanderer of my soul.

46. Detached from exterior things, dispossessed of

interior things, disappropriated of the things of God - neither will prosperity detain you nor adversity hinder you.

47. The devil fears a soul united to God as he does God himself. [26]

48. The purest suffering produces the purest understanding. [27]

49. The soul that desires God to surrender himself to it entirely must surrender itself entirely to him without keeping anything for itself.

50. The soul that has reached the union of love does not even experience the first motions of sin.

51. Old friends of God scarcely ever fail him, for they stand above all that can make them fail. [28]

52. My Beloved, all that is rugged and toilsome I desire for myself, and all that is sweet and delightful I desire for you.

53. What we need most in order to make progress is to be silent before this great God with our appetite and with our tongue, for the language he best hears is silent love. [29]

54. The submission [30] of a servant is necessary in seeking God. In outward things light helps to prevent one from falling; but in the things of God just the opposite is true: It is better for the soul not to see if it is to be more secure.

55. More is gained in one hour from God's good things than in a whole lifetime from your own.

56. Love to be unknown both by yourself and by others. Never look at the good or evil of others.

57. Walk in solitude with God; act according to the just measure; hide the blessings of God.

58. To lose always and let everyone else win is a trait of valiant souls, generous spirits, and unselfish hearts; it is their manner to give rather than receive even to the extent of giving themselves. They consider it a heavy burden to possess themselves, and it pleases them more to be possessed by others and withdrawn from themselves, since we belong more to that infinite Good than we do to ourselves.

59. It is seriously wrong to have more regard for God's blessings than for God himself: prayer and detachment.

60. Look at that infinite knowledge and that hidden secret. What peace, what love, what silence is in that divine bosom! How lofty the science God teaches there, which is what we call the anagogical acts that so enkindle the heart.

61. The secret of one's conscience is considerably harmed and damaged as often as its fruits are manifested to others, for then one receives as reward the fruit of fleeting fame.

62. Speak little and do not meddle in matters about which you are not asked.

63. Strive always to keep God present and to preserve within yourself the purity he teaches you.

64. Do not excuse yourself or refuse to be corrected by all; listen to every reproof with a serene countenance; think that God utters it.

65. Live as though only God and yourself were in this world, so that your heart may not be detained by anything human.

66. Consider it the mercy of God that someone occasionally speaks a good word to you, for you deserve none.

67. Never allow yourself to pour out your heart, even though it be but for the space of a Creed.

68. Never listen to talk about the weaknesses of others, and if someone complains of another, you can tell her humbly to say nothing of it to you.

69. Do not complain about anyone, or ask for anything; and if it is necessary for you to ask, let it be with few words.

70. Do not refuse work even though it seems that you cannot do it. Let all find compassion in you.

71. Do not contradict; by no means speak words that are not pure.

72. Let your speech be such that no one may be offended, and let it concern things that would not cause you regret were all to know of them.

73. Do not refuse anything you possess, even though you may need it.

74. Be silent concerning what God may have given you and recall that saying of the bride: My secret for myself [Is. 24:16].

75. Strive to preserve your heart in peace; let no event of this world disturb it; reflect that all must come to an end.

76. Take neither great nor little notice of who is with you or against you, and try always to please God. Ask him that his will be done in you. Love him intensely, as he deserves to be loved.

77. Twelve stars for reaching the highest perfection: love of God, love of neighbor, obedience, chastity, poverty, attendance at choir, penance, humility, mortification, prayer, silence, peace.

78. Never take others for your example in the tasks you have to perform, however holy they may be, for the devil will set their imperfections before you. But imitate Christ, who is supremely perfect and supremely holy, and you will never err.

79. Seek in reading and you will find in meditation; knock in prayer and it will be opened to you in contemplation.[31]

SAYINGS COLLECTED BY
SR. MAGDALENA DEL ESPIRITU SANTO [32]

1. He who works for God with pure love, not only takes no notice of whether men know his works or not, but does not even do things so that God himself should know them. One who acts like this, even if no one knows him, does not stop from doing this service, and he does it with the same joy and love.

2. Another maxim to help overcome the appetites: have a habitual desire to imitate Christ in all your doings by bringing your life into conformity with His. You must then study His life in order to know how to imitate Him and behave in all events as He would.

3. In order that you should be able to do this, renounce and remain empty of any sensory satisfaction that is not purely for the honor and glory of God. Do this out of love for Jesus Christ. In His life He had no other gratification, nor desire of any other, than the fulfillment of His Father's will, which He called His drink and food (Jn 4 34).

4. In order to mortify the four natural passions, which

are joy, sorrow, fear and hope act as follows;

> Endeavour to be inclined always
> not to the easiest,   but to the most difficult;
> not to the most delightful, but to the harshest;
> not to the most gratifying, but to the less pleasant;
> not to what means rest for you, but to hard work;
> not to the consoling, but to the unconsoling;
> not to the most, but to the less;
> not to the highest and most precious, but to the lowest
> and most despised;
> not to wanting something, but to wanting nothing.

Do not go about looking for the best of temporal things, but for the worst; and desire to be in complete nudity, emptiness, and poverty in everything in the world for the sake of Jesus Christ.[33]

5. On concupiscence:
    Try to act with contempt for yourself and desire that all others do likewise.
    Endeavour to speak in contempt of yourself and desire all others to do so.
    Try to think lowly and contemptuously of your self and desire that all others do the same.

6. Hold firm in your heart against everything that draws you towards anything which is not God; and for the sake of Christ love suffering.

7. Be prompt in obedience, take joy in suffering, mortify your sight, wish to know nothing, silence and hope.

8. Restrain your tongue and your thoughts and keep your heart always in God, and the Holy Spirit will give you enormous zeal. Read this often.

Sayings collected by Sr. Maria de Jesus [34]

1. Let your spirit rise up out of yourself without depending on anything.

2. Be always on guard over yourself without ever sleeping.

3. In your thoughts avoid others and close your door to everyone.

4. Be pure from all affections, thoughts and images, as you moan for a sweet song with contrition and tears.

OTHER COUNSELS

1. The further you withdraw from earthly things the closer you approach heavenly things and the more you find in God.

2. Whoever knows how to die in all will have life in all.

3. Abandon evil, do good, and seek peace [Ps. 34:14].

4. Anyone who complains or grumbles is not perfect, nor even a good Christian.

5. The humble are those who hide in their own nothingness and know how to abandon themselves to God.

6. The meek are those who know how to suffer their neighbour and themselves.

7. If you desire to be perfect, sell your will, give it to the poor in spirit, come to Christ in meekness and humility, and follow him to Calvary and the sepulchre.

8. Those who trust in themselves are worse than the devil.

9. Those who do not love their neighbor abhor God.

10. Anyone who does things lukewarmly is close to falling.

11. Whoever flees prayer flees all that is good.

12. Conquering the tongue is better than fasting on bread and water.

13. Suffering for God is better than working miracles.

14. Oh, what blessings we will enjoy in the vision of the Most Blessed Trinity!

15. Do not be suspicious of your brother, for you will lose purity of heart.

16. As for trials, the more the better.

17. What does anyone know who doesn't know how to suffer for Christ?

□

Celebration

The best way to become
familiar with God
is to celebrate Him.

To celebrate Him
means to exalt and applaud Him.
It means to toast a feast in his honour.

He deserves it.
Because His love is the greatest
and the most beautiful.
He is a never ending feast.

Celebration always involves others.
You cannot organise a feast alone.

God brings people together.

Here are some short celebrations in prayer.

The outline is very simple:
A song - a reading - quiet time- a reading -
a prayer - the Our Father - a song.

You can always add or deduct.
Creativity never did harm anyone.

Ten counsels on prayer

1. Always keep in mind that in everything you should walk in the footsteps of Jesus Christ. Build your life upon Him and Him alone. He loves you. Fall in love with Him.

2. The more you put your trust in things which interfere with prayer, the less will you have confidence in God; you cannot serve two masters!

3. The Father has said only one word: this was His Son. This Word is always present in eternal silence. It is only in silence that you can hear it.

4. Find therefore a place which is as deserted and quiet as possible, and there go to pray. Use all your strength and the joy of your will to call and to bless Him.

5. Remember that prayer is not thinking a lot, feeling a lot, moving a lot. Only one thing is necessary: to be willing to truly deny yourself for Him. To have many secrets of love with God. Otherwise all will collapse...

6. Be careful always to have your conscience clear, your will completely grounded in God and your mind totally drawn to God. The more simple you are, the more useful work you can do for the Church and for the world.

7. Faith, hope and love are able to draw us away from anything to unite us with God alone. There is no need for any other help in praying.

8. Who shuns away from prayer is running away from all that is good. For no reason whatsoever should you give up mental prayer for this is the strength of the soul. Do not rush in prayer. Do not lose heart ... ever.

9. There is no need to talk a great deal in prayer. There is no need to invent many ceremonies or techniques. It is enough what Jesus Christ taught us. This is what the Father listens to. Always. Therefore be simple: *When we come to prayer and other devotions, the souls must not, on their own whim, invent ceremonies and styles of prayer different from those which Jesus Christ taught us. It is clear that when the disciples asked Him to teach them how to pray, he taught them all that is necessary so that the Eternal Father would hear us - let's face it, He knows our tastes perfectly! Hence He only taught them the seven stanzas of the Our Father, which include all our needs, both spiritual and material, without teaching them any more words or ceremonies.*

10. *Let those who are very active and think that they will conquer the world with many sermons and much hustle-bustle of their own, realize that they will do more good to*

the Church and be more pleasing to God if they spend even half of this time before God in prayer, even if their prayer is not very perfect.

SAMPLE CELEBRATIONS

THEME I: *Let us live in perfect charity*
(Letter 19)

* **First reading**: A reading from the Gospel of Saint John (John 15, 7-11)

"If you remain in me and my words remain in you, ask whatever you wish, and it will be given you. This is to my Father's glory, that you bear much fruit, showing yourselves to be my disciples.

As the Father has loved me, so have I loved you. Now remain in my love. If you obey my commands, you will remain in my love, just as I have obeyed my Father's commands and remain in his love. I have told you this so that my joy may be in you and that your joy may be complete."

This is the word of the Lord!

* **Silence**

* **Second Reading**: A reading from the Spiritual
Canticle of Saint John of the Cross (Canticle 1,13)

"Where have you hidden,
Beloved, and left me moaning?

She calls him "Beloved" to move him more to
answer her prayer. When God is loved he very readily
answers the requests of his lover. This he teaches through
St. John: If you abide in me, ask whatever you want and it
shall be done unto you [Jn. 15:7]. You can truthfully call
God Beloved when you are wholly with him, do not allow
your heart attachment to anything outside of him, and
thereby ordinarily center your mind on him. This is why
Delilah asked Samson how he could say he loved her, since
his spirit was not with her [Jgs. 16:15], and this spirit
includes the mind and the affection.

Some call the Bridegroom beloved when he is not
really their beloved because their heart is not wholly set on
him. As a result their petition is not of much value in his
sight. They do not obtain their request until they keep their
spirit more continually with God through perseverance in
prayer, and their heart with its affectionate love more
entirely set on him. Nothing is obtained from God except
by love."

* **Silence** (Or canticle from Isaiah 66, 10-14 sung)

* **Spontaneous prayer** ending with the Our Father.

●

THEME II:●●   *Come Holy Spirit!*

* Song

* First reading: A reading from the first letter of Saint Paul to the Corinthians (1 Cor 13, 1-8.13)

"If I speak in the tongues of men and of angels, but have not love, I am only a resounding gong or a clanging cymbal. If I have the gift of prophecy and can fathom all mysteries and all knowledge, and if I have a faith that can move mountains, but have not love, I am nothing. If I give all I possess to the poor and surrender my body to the flames, but have not love, I gain nothing.

Love is patient, love is kind. It does not envy, it does not boast, it is not proud. It is not rude, it is not self-seeking, it is not easily angered, it keeps no record of wrongs. Love does not delight in evil but rejoices with the truth. It always protects, always trusts, always hopes, always perseveres.

Love never fails. But where there are prophecies, they will cease; where there are tongues, they will be stilled; where there is knowledge, it will pass away. And now these three remain: faith, hope and love. But the greatest of these is love."

This is the word of the Lord!

* Silence

* **Second reading**: A reading from the spiritual Canticle of St John of the Cross (Cant 13, 11-12)

Return, dove,
the wounded stag
is in sight on the hill,
cooled by the breeze of your flight.

By the "flight," he means the contemplation received in that ecstasy; and by the "breeze," the spirit of love that this flight of contemplation causes in the soul. He very appropriately terms this love caused by the flight a "breeze," because the Holy Spirit, who is love, is also compared to a breeze in Scripture, for the Holy Spirit is the breath of the Father and the Son. .... As a breeze cools and refreshes a person worn out by the heat, so this breeze of love refreshes and renews the one burning with the fire of love...

It is worthy of note that God does not place his grace and love in the soul except according to its desire and love. Those who truly love God must strive not to fail in this love, for they will thereby induce God, if we may so express it, to further love them and find delight in them. And to acquire this charity, one ought to practice what St. Paul taught: Charity is patient, is kind, is not envious, does no evil, does not become proud, is not ambitious, seeks not its own, does not become disturbed, thinks no evil, rejoices not in iniquity, but rejoices in the truth, suffers all things (that are to be suffered), believes all things (that must be believed), hopes all things, and endures all things (that are in accord with charity) [1 Cor. 13:4-7].

* **Silence** (or singing of Psalm 62)

* **Spontaneous prayer** ending with the Our Father.

* **Song**

●

THEME III: " *I Seek Your Face, O Lord!*

* **Song**

* **First reading**: A reading from the book of Exodus
(Ex 33 17-23)

" And the Lord said to Moses, 'I will do the very
thing you have asked, because I am pleased with you and I
know you by name'. Then Moses said, 'Now show me your
glory'. And the Lord said, 'I will cause all my goodness to
pass in front of you, and I will proclaim my name, the Lord,
in your presence. I will have mercy on whom I will have
mercy, and I will have compassion on whom I will have
compassion. But,' he said, 'you cannot see my face, for no
one may see me and live.' Then the Lord said, 'There is a
place near me where you may stand on a rock. When my
glory passes by, I will put you in a cleft in the rock and

cover you with my hand until I have passed by. Then I will remove my hand and you will see my back; but my face must not be seen.

This is the Word of the Lord!

* **Silence**

* **Second reading**: A reading from the Spiritual Canticle of Saint John of the Cross (Canticle 1, 10-11)

"However much the soul hides herself, she will never in this mortal life attain to so perfect a knowledge of these mysteries as she will possess in the next. Nevertheless, if like Moses she hides herself in the cavern of the rock (in real imitation of the perfect life of the Son of God, her Bridegroom), she will merit that, while he protects her with his right hand, God will show her his shoulders [Ex. 33:22-23], that is, he will bring her to the high perfection of union with the Son of God, her Bridegroom, and transformation in him through love....

You have been told, O soul, of the conduct you should observe if you want to find the Bridegroom in your hiding place. Still, if you want to hear this again, listen to a word abounding in substance and inaccessible truth: Seek him in faith and love, without desiring to find satisfaction in anything, or delight, or desiring to understand anything other than what you ought to know. Faith and love are like the blind person's guides. They will lead you along a path unknown to you, to the place where God is hidden. Faith, the secret we mentioned,is comparable to the feet by which one journeys to God, and love is like one's guide.

* **Song**

* **Silence** (or sing Psalm 30)

* **Spontaneous prayer** ending with the Our Father

* **Song**

●

THEME IV: *"In silence and hope"*

* **Song**

* **First reading**: A reading from the book of Hosea (Hos 2, 16.20-22)

"Therefore, behold, I shall allure her, and bring her into the wilderness, and speak tenderly to her heart. And I will give her, her vineyards, and the Valley of Achor will be for her a door of hope. And I will make for you a covenant on that day with the beasts of the field, the birds of the air, and creeping things of the ground; and I shall abolish the bow, the sword, and war from the land; and let them sleep secure.

And I will betroth you to Him for ever; I will betroth you to me in righteousness and in justice, in steadfast love, and in mercy I will betroth you to me in faithfulness; and you shall know the Lord".
This is the Word of the Lord!

* **Silence**

* **Second reading**: A reading from a letter of Saint John of the Cross (Letter 7)

"It is very necessary, my daughters, to hide the spirit from the devil and from our senses, for if we do not, we shall, without realizing it, find ourselves very backward and far from the virtues of Christ. Afterwards we shall awaken only to find our labour and work done in the wrong way, and thinking that we were carrying a lighted lamp, we shall discover that it has gone out. Because by blowing, in our opinion to keep it lighted, we perhaps did more to extinguish it.

I say, then, so that this might not happen, and that the spirit be preserved, that there is no better remedy than to suffer, to do, and to be silent and to close the senses through the inclination toward and practice of solitude and the forgetfulness of all creatures and happenings, even though the whole world crumbles.

Never, whether in adversity or in prosperity, cease

to quiet your heart with deep love so as to suffer whatever comes along. For perfection is so singularly important and the delight of the spirit is so high-priced that all of this is hardly enough to obtain it. It is impossible to advance without doing and suffering virtuously, all enveloped in silence.

Keep this in mind, daughters: the soul that is quick to turn to speaking and conversing is slow to turn to God. For when it is turned towards God, it is then strongly and inwardly drawn toward silence and flight from all conversation. For God desires a soul to rejoice with Him more than with any other person, however advanced and helpful the person may be.

Our greatest need is to be silent before this great God with the appetite and with the tongue, for the only language He hears is the silent language of love."

* **Silence** (or sing Psalm 130)

* **Spontaneous prayer** ending with the Our Father

* **Song**

●

THEME V: *"A mother's love"*

    * **Song**

    * **First reading**: A reading from the book of Isaiah (Is 66 10-14)

"Rejoice in Jerusalem, and be glad for her all you who love her; rejoice with her in joy, all you who mourn over her; that you may suck and be satisfied with her consoling breasts; that you may drink deeply with delight from the abundance of her glory.

For thus says the Lord: 'Behold I will extend prosperity to her like a river, and the wealth of the nations like an overflowing stream; and you shall suck, you shall be carried upon her hip, and dandled upon her knees as one whom his mother comforts, so I will comfort you; you shall be comforted in Jerusalem. You shall see, and your heart shall rejoice; your bones shall flourish like the grass; and it shall be known that the hand of the Lord is with his servants, and his indignation against his enemies." [35]

This is the Word of the Lord!

    * Silence

    * **Second reading**: A reading from the Dark Night of Saint John of the Cross (Dark Night 1, 2-3 & 12,1)

"It should be known, then, that God nurtures and caresses the soul, after it has been resolutely converted to His service, like a loving mother who comforts her child with the warmth of her bosom, nurses it with good milk and tender food, and carries it in her arms. But as the child grows older, the mother withholds her caresses and hides her tender love, she rubs bitter aloes on her sweet breasts and sets the child down from her arms, letting it walk on its own feet so that it may put aside the habits of childhood and grow accustomed to greater and more important things.

The grace of God acts just as a loving mother by re-engendering in the soul new enthusiasm and fervour in the service of God. With no effort on the soul's part, this grace causes it to taste sweet and delectable milk and to experience intense satisfaction in the performance of spiritual exercises, because God is handing the breast of His tender love to the soul, just as if it were a delicate child.

The soul finds its joy, therefore, in spending lengthy periods at prayer, perhaps even entire nights; its penances are pleasures; its faults happiness; and the sacraments and spiritual conversations are its consolations. Although spiritual persons do practice these exercises with great profit and persistence and are very careful about them, spiritually speaking, they conduct themselves in a very weak and imperfect manner. Since their motivation in their spiritual works and exercises is the consolations and satisfaction they experience in them, and since they have not been conditioned by the arduous struggle of practicing virtue, they possess many faults and imperfections in the discharge of their spiritual activities.

This glad night and purgation causes many benefits even though to the soul it seemingly deprives it of them. So numerous are these benefits that, just as Abraham made a great feast on the day of his son Isaac's weaning [Gn. 21:8], there is rejoicing in heaven that God has now taken from this soul its swaddling clothes; that he has put it down from his arms and is making it walk alone; that he is weaning it from the delicate and sweet food of infants and making it eat bread with crust; and that the soul is beginning to taste the food of the strong (the infused contemplation of which we have spoken), which in these sensory aridities and darknesses is given to the spirit that is dry and empty of the satisfactions of sense.

* **Silence** (or sing psalm 131)

* **Spontaneous prayer** ending with the Our Father

* **Song**

●

THEME VI: *"Christ the wisdom and power of God"*

* **Song**

* **First reading**: A reading from the first letter of St Paul to the Corinthians (1 Cor 11 7-25)

"For Christ did not send me to baptize but to preach the Gospel, and not with eloquent wisdom, lest the cross of Christ be emptied of its power. For the word of the cross is folly to those who are perishing, but to us who are being saved it is the power of God. For it is written: 'I will destroy the wisdom of the wise, and the cleverness of the clever I will thwart.' Where is the wise man? Where is the scribe? Where is the debater of this age? Has not God made foolish the wisdom of the world? For since, in the wisdom of God, the world did not know God through wisdom, it pleased God through the folly of what we preach to save those who believe. For Jews demand signs and Greeks seek wisdom, but we preach Christ crucified, a stumbling block to Jews and folly to Gentiles, but to those who are called, both Jews and Greeks, Christ is the power of God and the wisdom of God. For the foolishness of God is wiser than men, and the weakness of God is stronger than men."

This is the Word of the Lord!

* **Silence**

* **Second reading**: A reading from the writings of Saint John of the Cross (Ascent II 22, 5-6)

"God could respond as follows: If I have already told you all things in My Word, My Son, and if I have no other word, what answer or revelation can I now make that would surpass this?   Fasten your eyes on him alone, because in Him I have spoken and revealed all, and in Him you shall discover even more than you ask for and desire. You are making an appeal for locutions and revelations that are incomplete, but if you turn your eyes to Him you will find them complete. For He is My entire locution and response, vision and revelation,   which I have already spoken, answered, manifested, and revealed to you, by giving Him to you as a brother, companion, master, ransom and reward. Since that day when I descended upon Him with my Spirit on Mount Tabor proclaiming: "This is my Beloved Son in whom I am well pleased, hear Him", (Mt 17: 5), I have relinquished this method of answering and teaching, and presented them to Him.

Hear Him because I have no more faith to reveal nor truths to manifest. Behold Him well, for in Him you will uncover all these revelations already made, and many more. If you desire Me to answer with a word of comfort, behold my Son, subject to Me and to others out of love for Me, and you will see how much He answers. If you desire Me to declare some secret truths or events to you, fix your yes on Him, and you will discern hidden in Him the most secret mysteries and wisdom, and the wonders of God."

* Silence

* Spontaneous prayer (or the following litany may be said, based on the writing of Saint John of the Cross)

Christ, Son of God and Son of Man,
Christ, spotless mirror of the Eternal Father,
Christ, in whom the Father has said everything,
Christ, bottomless mine of divine treasures,
Christ, in whom are mysteries hidden indeed
        and treasures of divine wisdom,
Christ, manifestation of the Father,
Christ, beloved Son of the Father,
Christ, bridegroom of the Church,
Christ, bridegroom of faithful souls,
Christ, our God, humiliated and crucified,
Christ, our Redeemer,
Christ, Good Shepherd,
Christ, divine Master,
Christ, our life and our model,
Christ, our light,
Christ, door and life which unites us to God,
Christ, our brother and our companion,
Christ, our price and our prize,
Christ, beloved of the soul,
Christ, supreme good,
Christ, our destination,
Christ, all ours and all for us,

Have mercy on us

Have mercy on us

* Song

☐

Appendix

A word to pastoral workers

Saint John of the Cross and pastoral work today

What can a mystic who lived four hundred years ago tell us, pastoral workers, who struggle with today's problems, just before the third millennium? Obviously he is not going to offer us pastoral techniques but he can offer us a vision and an itinerary so that we can reach this vision. His word is important because it is experiential.

1. It is a fact that the religious climate is changing, indeed, in many ways, has already changed The process of de-christianisation is leaving its multifold effects; where before we could see God everywhere, now we see him nowhere. Yes many christians still remember God during the basic life-events like birth, marriage, death or in the unpleasant incidents of our lives: illness, natural disasters, accidents. But the need for God in our daily life is decreasing. He is no longer the motor that motivates our life. The computer has replaced Him!!

On the contrary, Saint John of the Cross seems to have God in his blood. *He was always talking about God,* witnesses said. He carried God with him. He remained known in the Church as the mystic *per antonomasia*. A mystic is a person who has an experience of God. God was not a vague feeling or an abstract idea for him, but someone intimate and close. *Outside God, everything is tasteless. God is everything.* John acquired a direction in his life which he would not change under any circumstances. This is why Saint John of the Cross can help us.

The emphasis must no longer be on devotionalism, which is a losing battle but on a solid experience of God. What are we to do so that we ourselves and others can have a true and profound encounter with Jesus Christ? The danger is that we escape into more rites. Saint John of the Cross was afraid of private revelations, visions, and Marian apparitions. *When God gave us his Son, his Word, the only Word He has spoken, in Him He told us everything at once and He has nothing more than Him to show us. Therefore, he who today wishes to ask or pray to the Lord for a vision or revelation is not only doing something stupid, but he is also offending God, because he is not fixing his eyes totally on Christ and is instead chasing after other things.*

Therefore we need more proclaiming of the kerygma. And a liturgy which is meaningful. An experience.

2 The Pope talks a great deal about *the second evangelization* because the effects of the first one appear to be weakening. In many countries, the old formulas which were traditionally used to transmit faith have become insufficient: a system based on the teaching of catechism to children, some catechesis on specific occasions like

baptism, first communion and confirmation and a homily once a week. This was a good system but today it does not answer the serious challenges which the secular culture is putting before the ordinary Christian. It is very urgent to create a new pedagogy of faith. Less religiosity and more faith. A need of Christian initiation.

The word of Saint John of the Cross is prophetic in this field. Even in his time he clearly attacked an over-saturation of religious practices and devotions which smother a true relationship with God because *it is like eating on a full stomach,* or *sowing on a land which is not tilled.*

It is necessary to evangelize those who are sacramentalised. Even in his writings, John avoided the usual themes to emphasize on the need of assimilating theological life. Knowledge and techniques are insufficient. One has to learn to digest; this is where the Magisterium of the Saint can be extremely relevant.

3. Progress in our society is ambivalent. We have developed many aspects of the personality of man but have neglected others. Man has become a machine: work, money, housework, office work, no time for anything, anxiety, depression. Production has become the crucial value of our society. We have condensed the ideal of man and we are now tasting the bitter fruit of this process: heart attacks, tranquilizers, drugs, the occult. This has caused a spiritual disorientation.

The mystical experience and the rich humanity of Saint John of the Cross open wide men's horizons, and restore their dignity. *The soul now prays for as much love as she had always wished for, because she who loves cannot be happy unless she is able to love so much as she is loved!* Man was not created for trivialities but for impressive things. God has a project for mankind and He wants to bring it to fruition with every individual. As soon as man puts God in the right place - that is the first place - he acquires an enormous potential to appreciate everything - yes everything.

Saint John of the Cross opens for us the windows which give out on the beauty and gratuitousness of God. The road he proposes leads to ... *the soul is as if always feasting, and from its mouth comes out a voice of divine joy like a new song full of joy and love.*

The beautiful reality is that this road is open to everyone.

Let it not be us, pastoral workers, who reduce the horizons of the Christians with whom we are working!

□

A word from Pope John Paul II

A short synthesis of the Apostolic Letter which Pope John Paul II issued on 14th December 1990 on the occasion of the opening of the celebrations of the fourth centenary of the death of St John of the Cross.

MASTER OF THE FAITH

Introduction

1. It is a great joy to the Church to see the great fruit of holiness and wisdom which her son Saint John of the Cross still produces. His example is an ideal for life; his writings are a treasure which should be shared with all those who today are seeking the face of God; his doctrine is a relevant word for today.

2. I myself felt drawn by the experience and teaching of the Saint of Fontiveros. From the first years of my priestly formation, I found in him a sure guide on the roads of faith.

3. By a beautiful coincidence he is our companion in our journey through this period of history, on the threshold of the year 2000, when we are celebrating the twenty fifth anniversary of the closure of the Second Vatican Council. A presence of God and of Christ, a filter which renews, under the guidance of the Holy Spirit, the experience of an enlightened and adult faith: is this really not the core of

the doctrine of Saint John of the Cross and his message for the Church and for mankind today? Renewing and awaking faith are without doubt the basis for facing every endeavor which now confronts the Church.

4. There are many aspects wherewith John of the Cross is known in the Church and in the world of culture. I want to look at his central message: the Living Faith - an escort for the Christian, a sole light in the dark night of trial, a burning flame fed by the Spirit.

I. Master of the Faith

The historical background

5. The Church at that time had many urgent commitments: a great Council - that of Trent - which revised doctrine and launched reform; a new continent, America, which had to be evangelized; an old world, Europe, which had to revitalize its Christian roots. The life of John of the Cross opens out in this historical background. He takes an open attitude.

6. John of Yepes answered to the grave spiritual needs of his time by embracing a contemplative vocation. By doing this, he is not evading responsibility; on the contrary... He shows how also the contemplative life is one way in which one can fulfill himself. His companions portray a dynamic image of John. Everything may be summarized in one profound conviction: *it is God and only God who gives value and taste to all endeavors.*

The commitment to form Christians

7. Brother John was an authentic formator of Christians. He knew how to initiate people to a familiar relationship with God, by teaching them to discover His presence and His love in the circumstances of life. He sought to create in his time an authentic pedagogy of faith by avoiding, on one hand, the danger of being too credulous and on the other hand, the danger of rigidity and lack of opening to the mystery.

Once these obstacles are overcome, the mystical doctor helps by his example and doctrine, to strengthen the faith with the basic qualities of that adult faith which Vatican Council II requires: a personal faith, which is free, convinced, grounded in the church, prayerful and adoring, - a solid committed faith. This is the faith which we need today.

II. A Witness of the living God

Depth and realism of his personal faith

8. John of the Cross is a lover of God. Before proclaiming and singing the mystery of God, he is God's witness, therefore he speaks of him with an unusual passion and persuasiveness. The witness proclaims what he has heard and seen.

Christ, the totality of revelation

9. His faith is so living and real because it is based on the central mysteries of Christianity. His preferred source of contemplation of these mysteries was the Eucharist ... and chapter 17 of St John's Gospel.

Dynamism of his theological life

10. One of the most valid contributions of Saint John of the Cross to Christian spirituality is his doctrine on the development of the theological life. Faith, linked to charity and hope, creates that intimate knowledge and perception which we call experience or sense of God. Christ appears to him as the beloved, indeed more as one who loves always more than before, as he sings in the poem El Pastorcico.

III. The ways of the life of faith

Faith and human existence

11. *The just man lives by faith.* His life is grounded on the faithfulness that God has towards his gifts and his promises; he lives committed to God's service in complete confidence. The mystical doctor speaks clearly about this. Among the aspects treated by the Saint, two have particular importance today for the life of the Christian: the relationship between human reason and faith, and the experience of faith through interior prayer.

12. One may be surprised that the doctor of the faith and of the dark night gives such great value to human reason. The Christian does not understand either why natural reason is despised in matters of faith or the opposition between human reason and the divine message.

13. Intellectual growth must pass through a development of the contemplative dimension of the Christian faith, fruit of the meeting with the mystery of God. It is precisely here that the major pastoral

preoccupations of the Spanish mystic stand forth. He invites us to live with the sight of faith and contemplative love, liturgy, the Word, divine images, the beauty of creation. He educates the soul to a simple way of interior union with Christ.

The dark night of faith and the silence of God

14. Our times have experienced dramatically the silence of God. The world of suffering. John of the Cross gives this experience the symbolic and evocative name of the dark night. Here he discovers something about the magnificent transformation which God brings about in the dark because *with wisdom and beauty he can give birth to good out of evil.*

15. The Doctor of the dark night brings out of this experience a pedagogy of the love of God. Even, in the experience of God's absence, He can communicate faith, hope and love.

Contemplation of Christ crucified

16. The silence of God has its strongest and clearest word when it communicates to us God's love in Christ crucified.

IV - A message of universal importance

Guide to those who seek God

17. Many are those who approach him attracted by the human values he represents. But he is also a guide for those who seek greater intimacy with God within the Holy Church. His teaching is indeed full of doctrine and life.

The theologian and the spiritual director can learn a lot from him.

Present day message to Spain, his country

18. For the profound, interior, national, cultural renewal which Spain needs today, John of the Cross offers the example of his life and the riches of his writing.

To the sons and daughters of Carmel

19. The ever greater interest that Saint John of the Cross is arousing among the people of our times is a motive of legitimate satisfaction for the children of the Discalced Carmel, of whom he is father, teacher and guide. Your vocation is a reason for great responsibility rather than for glory. What a blessing it would be if we were to find the word and the life of the saint made flesh and personified in every son of Carmel!

20. The saint dedicated the best of his apostolate and teaching to the Discalced Carmelite nuns. May they continue seeking with full commitment this pure and intimate love of God.

Conclusion

21. I invite everyone to listen to his witness to faith and to evangelical life. I recommend the work that will be done this year to our Redeemer and to Our Holy Mother.

□

© Lodge '96

FOOTNOTES

[1] Just before the centenary year 1990-1991, the Pope met a group of Spanish intellectuals and declared his admiration for this Saint explaining how relevant he is for the modern man: *John of the Cross, teacher of the faith, can be a real guide on the road of life. His word, always stimulating and profound, provokes in man an understanding of the fullness of his dignity as he searches an answer to the mystery of existence ... So, even today, in an age of many ambiguities, John of the Cross invites us to be men who seek for truth, people who walk by faith, people who place the truth of God above every human compromise .... this does not prevent the Christian from opening himself to the world around him. Indeed we may affirm that John of the Cross is the model of the Christian in dialogue with others.*

[2] This book would never have been published in English if it were not for the determination, insistence and hard work of **Mark Agius,** a medical doctor from Malta who now lives in England. A chance encounter led to a deep friendship. When he first read this book, he found it so stimulating that he translated it into English. His wife Ann typed the original manuscript. Then Mark started making the necessary contacts searching for a publishing house to edit and print this book, agents to promote it, persons to finance it... Quite a feat. His enthusiasm was really impressive and contagious. Please, keep Mark and Ann in your prayers.

[3] This is an adaptation of the main talk delivered during a Musico-Literary Evening held in honour of Saint John of the Cross in the Auberge de Provence, Valletta, Malta on April 4, 1991. The talk brings out the artistic genius of the Saint. This evening, which was organized by the Discalced Carmelite Friars and the National Association of Maltese Poets, was the concluding event to a national contest for poems on the Saint held during the centenary year commemorating the death of the Saint. The prizes were awarded by the then Minister of Education, now President of Malta, Dr. Ugo Mifsud Bonnici.

[4] You can see a synthesis of this Apostolic Letter in the Appendix at the end of the book.

[5] This is an excerpt from an article on Saint John of the Cross

which appeared in the Osservatore Romano.

⁶   In Spanish it sounds so powerful: *Oh noche que juntaste,*
   Amado con amada, Amada en el Amado trasformada!

⁷   See the third part of this book: His Writings.

⁸   The headings which accompany HIS LIFE are all taken from
the poems of Saint John of the Cross.

⁹   These new monks were called *Discalced Carmelites.*

¹⁰   Two years after his death, his body was taken to the town of
Segovia where it was venerated until, on 11th October 1927, it was
placed in a beautiful marble monument in the church of the Discalced
Carmelites. Pope Clement X declared him Blessed on 25th January
1675. Pope Benedict XIII declared him Saint on 26th December 1726.
On 24th August 1926 Pope Pius XI declared him a Doctor of the
universal church.

¹¹   See the whole prayer in part three of this book.

¹²   To show in a practical way the importance that the Saint attaches
to this project of divine union, a study has been made on the Saint's
choice of words and it was found that the word *union* appears more
than five hundred times in his writing. If we then add words with similar
meaning such as 'to join, to change, to resemble', we then find that he
uses the concept union more than a thousand times. In other words,
the saint uses this word on purpose. The following stanzas include all
the doctrine I intend to discuss in this book, The Ascent of Mount
Carmel. They describe the way that leads to the summit of the mount
- that high state of perfection we here call union of the soul with God.
(Ascent - Prologue)

¹³   Phillipians 2, 5-11

¹⁴   See also Canticle 37,3 and 23, 3-6. Although it is true that the
oriental mystics have a vision somewhat similar to that of John of the
Cross, there is a huge difference between them. Saint John of the Cross
is a Christian, and so his vision has historic roots, for our God is a
historic God - God who created and God who saves. While religion is
the attempt of man to reach and approach God, faith is the attempt by
God to reach man, heal the deep wounds caused by sin and gently
draw man to Himself for all eternity. This is the line the saint takes.

¹⁵   Perhaps the book in which this vision is most clear is the
Spiritual Canticle.

¹⁶   I wish to write this sentence in Spanish, for it acquires more

beauty and more force: *Yo soy tuyo y para ti - y gustar ser tal cual soy - para ser tuyo - y para darme a ti!!*

[17] These sentences are all collected in the third part of this book.

[18] We are fortunate that we have this small notebook of 22 pages which collect these 76 Maxims handwritten by Saint John of the Cross. It is dedicated to Madre Francisca de la Madre de Dios, a Carmelite nun of Beas. It is called the autograph of Andujar because it is kept in the Church of Santa Maria la Mayor in Andujar (Jaen). The prologue is not found in this autograph, but in another copy called the Codex of Burgos. We are here using the translation of Kavanaugh and Rodriguez - ICS version. We have only changed the numbers to reflect more the original

[19] In Spanish *cornadillo* is a diminutive of the smallest coin used at the time - the *cornado*.

[20] This **Prayer of a Soul taken by Love** has a truly remarkable poetic and mystic expression. These is a strong *crescendo* from nothing to the All. The soul first recognizes its nothingness due to sin, it realizes how impossible it is to approach God but she fills herself with hope as she looks towards God. She realizes how much she has received from Jesus Christ and bursts into a Song of praise and of total union.

[21] This sentence is often interpreted as referring simply to the end of our life: *"in the evening of life"*. The thought of the Saint is wider; in the end of life, or of every day, after each work you do, great or small, after each deed or omission, you will be judged on the quality of your love of God. It is not the results which count but the heart you put into what you do. Indeed, God reasons very differently from man!

[22] Here are eighty more sentences which were first published in 1646. Some are sentences taken from the preaching or conferences given by the Saint. They are full of vitality, doctrine and common sense. To understand their full meaning they must be read in the light of the whole of the Saint's message.

[23] *Advertencia amorosa de Dios* - a look full of attention and love towards God. This is what the Christian is according to the Saint John of the Cross. This is where he wants to lead us to. Would that we arrive there ... quickly!

[24] See Ascent 1 chapter 6 to 10 where the Saint in a strong psychological way depicts a clear picture of man's conditioning imprisoned by his appetites. We are called to freedom not slavery.

[25] *Pajaro solitario* - the sparrow mentioned in Psalm 102, 8. See The Spiritual Canticle, 14-15. We have the testimony of Sister Isabel

de la Encarnacion who stated that the saint wrote a small booklet called **Propriedades del pajaro solitario** *in which he described the meaning of silence and love of heaven which the soul should have in its journey to perfection.* This book is lost.

[26] See Canticle 24, 4

[27] See Canticle 36, 12-13.

[28] See Canticle 25, 9-11.

[29] See his beautiful **letter** n° 8, dated 22nd November 1587 to the Carmelites of Beas.

[30] In Spanish, *desancillar.* Some translate this way: *Be simple when you seek God.*

[31] This is a literal translation of the Carthusian Guido: Quaerite legendo et invenietis meditando; pulsate orando, et aprietur vobis contemplando. See Scala Paradisi, c 2 PL 40, 998.

[32] We have the autograph copy of this Carmelite nun. She was the first of the Carmelite nuns of Beas to begin to go to confession to the Saint. She was professed in 1577, in 1589 she was sent for the foundation of the monastery in Cordoba, she died in 1640. Her testimony on the Saint is very rich. She was the nun who was commissioned to copy his poems after his escape from the Toledo prison. It was to her that he dedicated the drawing of The Ascent of Mount Carmel. We even have an autograph copy of the ten sentences written by the saint with a dedication which says: *Jhs. Madalena del Spu. Sancto.*

[33] See 1 Ascent 13,3 where he expounds very well these ten sentences.

[34] Maria de Jesus (de Solis y Mendoza) was prioress of the Discalced Carmelite nuns of Salamanca. She made her profession on 2nd January 1600 and died on 9th January 1642. In 1623 she was healed miraculously by the Saint. A canonical process took place to verify this healing.

[35] This was one of Saint Theresa of the Child Jesus' favourite pages of the Scripture. She is rightly considered the greatest disciple of Saint John of the Cross in our own time.

□

Further copies of this book can be obtained from good
Christian book shops or direct from the Distributors:

New Life Renewal Services
60 Wickstead Avenue
Luton, Beds. LU4 9DP
Tel: 01582 571010

Complete book list sent on request